FRESH **ITALIAN** COOKING

FRESH
ITALIAN
COOKING

The Taunton Press

The Taunton Press
Inspiration for hands-on living®

The Taunton Press, Inc.
63 South Main Street
PO Box 5506, Newtown, CT 06470-5506
e-mail: tp@taunton.com

Translations:

Catherine Howard - Mary Doyle - John Venerella
Salvatore Ciolfi for Rosetta Translations SARL - Rosetta Translations SARL

LIBRARY OF CONGRESS CATALOGING-IN-PUBLICATION DATA IN PROGRESS

ISBN: 978-1-62113-812-9

Printed in China

10 9 8 7 6 5 4 3 2 1

EDITED BY

ACADEMIA BARILLA

INTRODUCTION

GIANLUIGI ZENTI

TEXT

CHEF MARIO GRAZIA

MARIAGRAZIA VILLA

GIOVANNI GANDINO

LORENA CARRARA

PHOTOGRAPHS

ALBERTO ROSSI

ACADEMIA BARILLA EDITORIAL COORDINATION

ILARIA ROSSI
CHATO MORANDI
REBECCA PICKRELL

GRAPHIC DESIGN

MARIA CUCCHI

CONTENTS

LIST OF RECIPES

Promoting Italian Gastronomic Culture around the World

Academia Barilla, like the land where it was born, has a vocation it believes in. Its headquarters is pleasant and functional. Its employees demonstrate specific skills relating to the culinary art of which it is an ambassador.

Academia Barilla's modern, international center dedicated to the dissemination of Italian cuisine is located in Parma, the very heart of the Food Valley. It is a city that enjoys worldwide recognition as a major center of culinary art. Indeed, not only does it boast a *gourmand* way of life, an ancient tradition of agriculture and high quality food in general, but it is also the home of some of the best-known typical Italian products: from Parmigiano-Reggiano cheese to Parma ham, Culatello to numerous salami specialties, and many different types of pasta.

Academia Barilla was founded in 2004 and built on the location where the historic Barilla pasta factory had stood, inside the new Barilla Center designed by Renzo Piano. It provides training courses, services and products of excellence to promote Italian gastronomic culture to both professionals and food lovers alike. With the objective of defending and protecting the Italian culinary heritage from imitations and counterfeits, Academia Barilla promotes the distribution of high-quality products that derive from ancient knowledge and practices, and appraises, through significant investments and the creation of dedicated services, the role of Italian restaurants and restaurant services around the world.

Designed to meet training requirements for the food industry, the facilities of Academia Barilla consist of a spectacular gourmet auditorium surrounded by a sensory analysis lab; several rooms for classroom teaching and hands-on training sessions that are equipped with the latest technology; an internal restaurant; and a well-endowed library dedicated to gastronomy, which, thanks to over 10,000 volumes and the historical collections of menus and culinary prints, protects tradition while at the same time blending it with innovation.

Academia Barilla offers a large number of training courses organized according to content as well as the level of skill required. A team of professional chefs and visiting chefs of international renown, such as Moreno Cedroni, Scott Conant, Carlo Cracco, Alfonso Iaccarino, Giada De Laurentiis and Giancarlo Perbellini, make up the Academia Barilla teaching staff. These are qualified chefs who can offer special and unique opportunities ranging from personalized guidance to rapid courses, from theme meetings to a classical *lectio magistralis*.

Academia Barilla is a point of reference with regard to providing services to businesses. It of-

ACADEMIA BARILLA

fers the opportunity to organize gastronomic, culinary or food-related press conferences and product presentations; incentive programs; meetings and conventions; team building programs; thematic seminars, conferences, and training courses with high standards for quality and presentation.

Memorable gourmet tours, customized by way of itinerary and duration to explore and discover more about Italy's enological, gastronomical and cultural traditions, are a fundamental aspect of the mission of Academia Barilla. Enjoy unforgettable landscapes and encounters with haute cuisine, excursions to the locations where renowned local specialties are produced and to famous wine cellars, dinners in enchanting castles and stately homes, concerts and high-end musical events, shopping in the most exclusive Italian fashion and designer shops, time to relax in splendid spas and elegant resorts.

Academia Barilla also organizes cultural events and promotional initiatives for the dissemination of culinary knowledge that are open to the general public, with the participation of experts, chefs, and food critics.

The Academia Barilla center in Parma also distributes, under its own name, a range of high-quality Italian specialties, produced by small nonindustrial companies and selected by accredited chefs and expert restaurateurs: aged cheese (Parmigiano-Reggiano DOP, Pecorino Toscano DOP, Pecorino Sardo Gran Cru and Pecorino Dolce), Parma ham, extra virgin olive oils from various Italian regions, traditional balsamic vinegar of Modena, artisan compotes (Chianti wine jelly, spicy fig compote, hand-cut fresh pears with balsamic vinegar) and sea salt from Sicily (flavored with black olives or fresh orange peel) are among the products selected for export.

In addition, Academia Barilla promotes the "Premio Cinema" (Film Award) for documentaries on Italian traditions related to food. In 2007, Academia Barilla was awarded the "Premio Impresa-Cultura" (Company-Culture Award) for its efforts in promoting the Italian spirit and Italian creativity around the world.

All of Academia Barilla's cultural heritage is featured in its website www.academiabarilla.com. You can search online for books in the Gastronomic Library; the collections of prints and menus and hundreds of historical texts have all been scanned or digitized and indexed for online searching and browsing.

GIANLUIGI ZENTI

BREADS & SMALL PLATES

CHAPTER ONE

OLIVE BREADSTICKS
FILONCINI ALLE OLIVE

Preparation time: 1 hour and 30 minutes + 20-25 minutes cooking time

Ingredients for 10 servings

all-purpose flour   4 cups (500 g)
water   1 cup (250 ml)
brewer's yeast   1/2 oz (15 g)
salt   1 1/2 tsp (10 g)
sugar   3 1/2 tsp (15 g)
pitted green olives, roughly chopped
  3 1/2 oz (100 g) about 23 large
extra-virgin olive oil   3 tbsp + 2 tsp
  (50 ml)

Difficulty

Method

Mix the flour, water, oil and yeast. Dissolve the salt in a few drops of water and add it to the mix. Knead the dough for a few minutes, then add the olives (roughly chopped). Cover the dough with a cloth and let it rise in a warm place for 20 minutes.

Divide it into pieces of equal size and shape them into breadsticks (you should get about 10). Arrange in a pan lined with parchment paper and let rise in a warm place until they've doubled in size.

Bake a preheated oven at 400° F (200° C) until golden brown and crispy, about 20-25 minutes, depending on the size of the breadsticks.

A THOUSAND TYPES OF BREAD

If Italy is the country of "a hundred cities" and "a thousand bell towers," then there are even more traditional breads to be enjoyed. This food, simultaneously simple and complex, has historically taken on many forms. Though it remains universally recognizable as "bread," it always manifests itself in different flavors with different features. Depending on the socio-economic conditions of where it is produced, the ritual meaning connected to it, and the intended culinary use, bread can be large or small, white or black, tapered, ring-shaped, braided, or an infinite number of other shapes. The creativity of the Italian people has resulted in many different forms of bread, from the basic loaf (whose semi-spherical shape seems to fit the curve of your hands) to longer shapes (probably a nod to pagan fertility symbols), to the ring shape that recalls a sun disk. Bread still plays a cultural, magical, recreational, and convivial role that is unparalleled.

EXTRA-VIRGIN OLIVE OIL BREADSTICKS IN THREE FLAVORS
GRISSINI ALL'OLIO EXTRA-VERGINE DI OLIVA AI TRE SAPORI

Preparation time: 20 minutes + 1 hour to rise + 7-8 minutes cooking time

Ingredients for 4 servings

soft wheat flour (preferably Italian-type flour)   4 cups (500 g)
brewer's yeast   1 oz (30 g)
extra-virgin olive oil   3 tbsp + 2 tsp (50 ml)
water   1 cup (250 ml)
fresh rosemary, finely chopped   1 oz (30 g) about 1 cup
sun-dried tomatoes, finely chopped   3 tbsp (20 g)
black olives, finely chopped   3/4 oz (20 g)
sugar   1 3/4 tsp (7 g)
cornmeal or semolina   as needed
salt   1 1/2 tsp (10 g)

Method

Dissolve the yeast in 2/3 cup (150 ml) water. Combine with the flour, remaining water, sugar and oil. Dissolve the salt in a few drops of water and add it at the very end. Divide the dough into 3 equal pieces. Mix the rosemary into 1 piece, the sun-dried tomatoes into another and the olives into the third. Cover them each in plastic wrap and let them rise in a warm place until they double in size.

Cut each one into pieces as thick as your finger. Dip them in cornmeal or semolina and stretch them into breadsticks (long or short as you prefer) by hand.

Place them in a pan lined with parchment paper and immediately bake in a preheated oven at 500° F (260° C) until golden brown and crispy, about 7-8 minutes.

THE MYSTERIOUS ORIGINS OF BREADSTICKS

Legends about the origins of a particular food often pop up after it's become popular. This was the case for breadsticks, a new stick-shaped bread from Piedmont. It seems that the invention, or at least the popularity of breadsticks is linked to the history of the House of Savoy. Young Vittorio Amedeo II (17th century) was in poor health and often suffered from fevers and intestinal disturbances. The court doctors, in keeping with the dietary principles of the time, attributed these problems to the consumption of partially raw bread. So the bakers were asked to produce a new kind of bread: light, pure, healthy, and well cooked, almost like a hard cookie.
But it's more likely that breadsticks, or grissini, are simply an extreme version of gherrsa or grissia, a traditional Piedmontese bread, similar to the baguette that's still so popular in France. One thing is definite – breadsticks were long reserved for aristocratic tables only.

Difficulty

OREGANO CRACKERS
CRACKER ALL'ORIGANO

Preparation time: 10 minutes + 50 minutes rising time + 15 minutes cooking time

Ingredients for 10 servings

soft wheat flour   8 cups (1 kg)
water   2 1/3 cups (550 ml)
dried or fresh oregano   1 tbsp (5 g)
fresh yeast   1 tbsp + 2 tsp (20 g)
extra-virgin olive oil   3 tbsp + 2 tsp
   (50 ml)
salt   1 tbsp (20 g)

Method

Put the oregano (dried or fresh, the amount can vary considerably depending on the intensity of the aroma) in the oil.

Dissolve the yeast in the water, heated to 85-95° F (30-35° C).

Make a well with flour on a work surface. Add the dissolved yeast to the center of the well and gradually incorporate the flour. Knead until the dough begins to take shape, then add the oil with the oregano. Lastly, add the salt and continue to knead until the dough is soft, smooth and elastic.

Cover the dough with plastic wrap and let rest for about 10 minutes.

Roll out the dough with a rolling pin to a thickness of about 1/25 inch (1 mm). Cut the crackers into shapes of your choice with a fluted pastry wheel and arrange in a baking pan lined with parchment paper. Cover with plastic wrap and set in a warm place. Let rise for about 40 minutes.

Before baking, prick the crackers with a fork to keep them from swelling up during cooking.

Bake in the oven at 350° F (180° C) until golden, about 15 minutes.

Difficulty

SUN-DRIED TOMATO AND CAPER TWISTS

NASTRINE CON POMODORI SECCHI E CAPPERI

Preparation time: 1 hour + 1 hour and 30 minutes rising time + 20 minutes cooking time

Ingredients for 4 servings

FOR THE DOUGH:
soft wheat flour   4 cups (500 g)
egg   1
sugar   1 tbsp + 2 tsp (20 g)
fresh yeast   1 tbsp + 2 tsp (20 g)
water   1 cup (250 ml)
salt   2 tsp (12 g)
**unsalted butter, softened to room
   temperature**   2 tbsp (25 g)

FOR THE FILLING:
sun-dried tomatoes, chopped   2 1/8 oz
   (60 g)
capers, rinsed and desalted
   5 1/3 oz (150 g)
egg, beaten   1
oregano   to taste

Method

Make a well in the flour on a work surface. Add the sugar, the egg and combine, adding, little by little, the water, into which you will have dissolved the yeast. Add the softened butter and the salt and knead until the dough is soft, smooth and elastic.

Cover the dough with plastic wrap and let rise for about 30 minutes in a warm, humid place.

Meanwhile, chop the sun-dried tomatoes, mix with the capers and add oregano to taste, set aside.

Roll the dough on a floured work surface with a rolling pin to a thickness of about 1/8 inch (3 mm). Brush the surface with some of the beaten egg and cover with the chopped sun-dried tomato, caper, and oregano mixture. Fold the sheet of dough in two to enclose the filling and cut it into 1 1/2-inch (3 cm) wide strips. Wind the strips into twists and place them on a baking tray greased with butter.

Let them rise again for about an hour, until they double in size.

Brush the twists with the remainder of the beaten egg and bake in the oven at 400° F (200° C) until golden brown, about 20 minutes.

Difficulty

PARMESAN BUNS
GIRANDOLE AL PARMIGIANO-REGGIANO

Preparation time: 1 hour + 1 hour and 30 minutes rising time + 20 minutes cooking time

Ingredients for 4 servings

FOR THE DOUGH:
soft wheat flour   4 cups (500 g)
egg   1
sugar   1 tbsp + 2 tsp (20 g)
fresh yeast   1 tbsp + 2 tsp (20 g)
water   1 cup (250 ml)
salt   2 tsp (12 g)
**unsalted butter, softened to room
  temperature**   2 tbsp (25 g)

FOR THE FILLING:
Parmigiano-Reggiano cheese, grated
  2/3 cup (60 g)
egg, beaten   1

Method

Make a well in the flour on a work surface. Add the sugar, the egg and combine, adding, little by little, the water, into which you will have dissolved the yeast. Add the softened butter and the salt and knead until the dough is soft, smooth and elastic.

Cover the dough with plastic wrap and let rise for about 30 minutes in a warm, humid place.

Roll the dough on a floured work surface with a rolling pin to a thickness of about 1/8 inch (3 mm). Brush the surface with some of the beaten egg and cover with the grated Parmigiano cheese. Twist the sheet of pastry into a rope approximately 3/4-inch (2 cm) thick, and cut into four pieces and roll each rope into a bun.

Place them on a baking tray greased with butter and let them rise again for about an hour, until they double in size.

Brush the surface of the buns with the remaining beaten egg and bake in the oven at 400° F (200° C) until golden brown, about 20 minutes.

Difficulty

FRIED PIZZA FROM MESSINA

PIZZA FRITTA MESSINESE

Preparation time: 30 minutes + 1 hour and 30 minutes rising time + 5 minutes cooking time

Ingredients for 4 servings

FOR THE DOUGH:

soft wheat flour (preferably Italian-type flour) 2 4/5 cups (350 g)
durum wheat flour 1 cup (150 g)
water 1 1/8 cups (270 ml)
lard, softened at room temperature
  1 3/4 oz (50 g)
fresh yeast 2 tbsp + 2 tsp (40 g)
salt 1 2/3 tsp (10 g)
oil for frying

FOR THE FILLING:

escarole, chopped 1 head
anchovies, chopped 6
cherry tomatoes, quartered 10
Caciocavallo cheese, diced 3 1/2 oz
  (100 g)
extra-virgin olive oil 2 tbsp (30 ml)
salt and pepper to taste

Method

Mix the two types of flour and make a well in the flour mixture on a work surface. Dissolve the yeast in 2/3 cup (150 ml) water at room temperature or, alternatively, crumble it directly onto the flour mixture. Knead the flour together with the softened lard, and the dissolved yeast. Dissolve the salt in 3 tablespoon + 1 teaspoon of water and knead into the dough.

Cover the dough in plastic wrap and let rise in a warm, humid place until doubled in size, about 1 hour.

In the meantime, prepare the filling. Wash and dry the escarole, chop it into strips and toss in a large bowl with the oil, salt, pepper, quarered cherry tomatoes, diced Caciocavallo cheese and the chopped anchovies. Set aside.

Divide the dough into pieces of approximately 3 1/2 oz (100 g) each, and roll into balls between the palms of your hands. Cover the balls of dough in plastic wrap and let rise in a warm, humid place until doubled in size, about 1/2 hour.

On a work surface, use a rolling pin to flatten the balls of dough into disks. Spread about a tablespoon of filling to cover half the surface of each disk, fold the dough into a half-moon shape over the filling and press or use the tines of a fork to seal the edges. Heat about 1/2 inch of oil in a pan until hot, and fry the half-moons a few at a time until they are lightly golden, about 5 minutes. Remove them from the pan with a slotted spoon, place on paper towels to drain and season with a pinch of salt. Serve immediately.

Difficulty

TOMATO JELLY WITH BURRATA CHEESE AND PESTO
GELATINA DI POMODORO CON BURRATA E PESTO

Preparation time: 30 minutes + 2 hours to set

Ingredients for 4 servings

ripe tomatoes   2.2 lbs (1 kg) about
   5 1/2 large
burrata cheese   3 1/2 oz (100 g)
gelatin sheets   4-5
salt and pepper   to taste

PESTO:

basil leaves   1 cup packed (15 g) about
   30 leaves
Parmigiano-Reggiano cheese, grated
   1/3 cup (30 g)
Pecorino cheese, grated   3 tbsp (20 g)
pine nuts   1 tbsp (8 g)
extra-virgin olive oil, preferably Ligurian
   1/3 cup + 2 tbsp (100 ml)
garlic clove   half

Method

Wash and dry the basil. Combine basil, garlic, Parmigiano-Reggiano, Pecorino, and pine nuts in a mortar and crush them all together. Transfer to a larger bowl and gradually whisk in olive oil until the mixture is creamy and emulsified.

Peel the tomatoes and remove the seeds. Pass them through a vegetable mill or purée them in a food processor and season them with salt and pepper to taste.

Heat part of the tomato purée in a pan. Soak the gelatin in cold water, then add it to the heated tomato purée and let it dissolve. Add the rest of the tomato purée and pour it into glasses. Refrigerate for at least 2 hours.

Once the tomato jelly has set, top with a spoonful of burrata, garnish with pesto, and serve well chilled.

Difficulty

TOMATO-BASIL BRUSCHETTA
BRUSCHETTA CON POMODORO E BASILICO

Preparation time: 20 minutes

Ingredients for 4 servings

baguette   14 oz (400 g) about 1
tomatoes, diced, preferably San Marzano
   10 1/2 oz (300 g) about 2 large
extra-virgin olive oil   1 tbsp + 1 tsp
   (20 ml)
basil leaves, roughly chopped   4
garlic clove   1
salt   to taste

Method

Slice the bread into pieces about 1/3- to 1/2-inch (1-cm) thick and toast them in the oven or in a pan on the stove. Once they're toasted, peel the garlic and lightly rub it over the bread.

Dice the tomatoes and mix in a bowl with the oil, salt and roughly chopped basil. Let it sit for a few minutes for the flavors to absorb. Spread some of the diced tomato mixture on top of each bread slice and serve.

RUSTIC BREAD

In the past, many people made their bread at home using coarsely ground whole grain flours and natural yeast made through a long and precise treatment applied to already leavened bread. The bacteria responsible for this leavening gave the bread an unmistakable aroma. The higher acidity of starters, compared to modern yeast, made the bread more resistant to further contamination by bacteria and therefore made it more "preservable," which is why bread once lasted much longer. This explains why loaves of rustic country bread were so incredibly large, but there are other factors that played into the size and shape of bread. First there were socio-economic factors. On the other hand, if the families did not have their own ovens the loaves tended to be larger in order to reduce dependence on local lords.

Difficulty

CAPRESE WITH BASIL
CAPRESE CON BASILICO

Preparation time: 25 minutes + 15 minutes cooking time

Ingredients for 4 servings

buffalo-mozzarella cheese   3/4 lb (320 g)
tomatoes   1/2 lb (250 g)
basil, fresh   3/8 oz (10 g)
extra-virgin olive oil   3 1/2 tbsp (50 ml)
salt   scant tsp or 1/5 oz (5 g)
pepper   scant tsp or 1/8 oz (2 g)

Method

Slice the tomatoes and the mozzarella.

Place slices of tomato and mozzarella alternately on a plate. Season with salt and pepper to taste.

Finally, decorate with fresh basil leaves and drizzle with olive oil.

Difficulty

CHEF'S TIPS

This dish is best in the summertime when fresh vegetables are plentiful.

PANZANELLA

PANZANELLA

Preparation time: 15 minutes

Ingredients for 4 servings

stale rustic Tuscan bread   2.2 lbs (1 kg)
anchovies, finely chopped   1 oz (30 g)
tomatoes, diced   7 oz (200 g) about 2
seedless cucumber, diced   4 1/5 oz
   (120 g) about 1 small
onions, diced   5 1/3 oz (150 g) about
   2 small
bell peppers, diced   1/2 lb (250 g)
   about 2 medium
garlic clove, minced   1
capers, well rinsed and finely chopped
   1 tbsp (8 g)
fresh basil leaves   20
red wine vinegar   1 tbsp (15 ml)
extra-virgin olive oil, preferably Tuscan
   1/4 cup + 2 tbsp (80 ml)
salt   1/2 tsp (3 g)
black pepper   to taste

Difficulty

Method

Cut the bread into 3/4 inch (2 cm) cubes, leaving the crust on. Finely chop the garlic with the anchovies and capers and put them all in a large bowl. Add the salt, freshly ground pepper, vinegar and oil and mix well. Dice the vegetables and add them along with the bread to the garlic/anchovie mixture. Mix again, making sure everything is coated with the dressing, and season with salt and pepper to taste. Add few leaves of basil to garnish. Panzanella is even tastier if you make it the day before and refrigerate it overnight to let all the flavors meld.

BREAD CIVILIZATION

It is no coincidence that farming culture was defined as a "bread civilization." This food can probably be considered the first complex gastronomic product in human history, and it is a universal symbol of the incalculable distance between Homo sapiens and other creatures, which are limited to naturally occurring nourishment they cannot modify. Homer defined humans as "bread eaters," as though this seemingly simple foodstuff encompassed all that is meant by "civilization." In the past, therefore, bread was looked upon with an almost sacred respect, also due to the fact that in a subsistence economy, like that of the ancient Mediterranean region, nothing could be wasted. Children were actually forbidden to play with it and break it up into crumbs at the table. It was considered very bad luck to place it on the table upside down. Since Catholics equated bread to the Christ figure, a cross was often cut into the top of bread loaves, both for religious purposes and to facilitate rising. Anyone who threw away bread was actually condemned to a terrible punishment. These few examples illustrate the historic and anthropological origins of the many Italian dishes that reuse and reinterpret stale bread, in a sort of gastronomic rebirth that is still highly appreciated today.

SARDINIAN SUMMER NURAGHE
INSALATA CON PANE CARASAU

Preparation time: 30 minutes

Ingredients for 4 servings

Carasau bread   6 slices
cherry tomatoes, thinly sliced   5 1/3 oz
  (150 g)
shallots   5 1/3 oz (150 g)
radishes, sliced thin   5 1/3 oz (150 g)
cucumbers, sliced thin   5 1/3 oz (150 g)
extra-virgin olive oil   2 tbsp (30 ml)
Pecorino cheese, slivers   3 oz (90 g)
fresh chives, for garnish
salt and black pepper   to taste

Method

Carasau bread is a flat bread from Sardinia. Dip the bread into a bowl of water until it starts to soften. When the bread has softened, cut it into 16 squares or circles with a diameter of 2 to 3 inches.

Season all the vegetables with salt and pepper to taste and drizzle with a little of the oil.

Place one Carasau round in the center of a plate. Arrange tomato slices on top of the round bread in one layer, overlapping them slightly. Top with another cracker (Carasau) and arrange radish slices on top in the same manner. Top with another round and a layer of cucumber slices and shallots, followed by another cracker. Arrange the Pecorino on top and around the stack.

Drizzle remaining olive oil over the stack and on the plate and sprinkle the plate with the chopped chives.

Difficulty

DID YOU KNOW THAT...

Pane Carasau is also known as "carta musica" (music sheet) due to its resemblance to the parchment that sacred music was written on.

TOMATOES STUFFED WITH RICE

POMODORI RIPIENI DI RISO

Preparation time: 20 minutes + 20 minutes cooking time

Ingredients for 4 servings

extra-virgin olive oil   1/4 cup (60 ml)
vine-ripened tomatoes   4
**short-grained rice, such as Roma or
   Sant'Andrea**   1/2 cup (100 g)
oregano   3 1/2 tbsp (20 g)
basil leaves   4
garlic clove   half
salt   to taste

Method

Boil the rice in 1 cup salted water for 10 minutes. Drain it and let it cool.

Cut the tops off the tomatoes and hollow them out. Finely chop the pulp you removed, along with the oregano, basil and garlic. Season the mixture with oil and salt to taste, then stir it into the rice.

Fill the tomatoes with the rice mixture, put the tops back on and arrange in a pan lined with aluminum foil.

Bake in a preheated oven at 325° F (160° C) for about 15-20 minutes. Let cool and then refrigerate for a few hours. Serve cold.

Difficulty

SAVORY BREAD PUDDING
SFORMATO DI PANE CASERECCIO

Preparation time: 20 minutes + 20 minutes cooking time

Ingredients for 4 servings

rustic bread, cubed, crusts removed
 3 cups (100 g)
extra-virgin olive oil   1 tbsp + 1 tsp
 (20 ml)
shallots, chopped   2 tbsp (20 g)
Caciocavallo cheese, diced   2 oz (60 g)
porcini mushrooms   3 1/2 oz (100 g)
minced parsley   1/4 cup (20 g)
whole milk   1/2 cup (125 ml)
egg   1
Parmigiano-Reggiano cheese   1/3 cup
 (30 g)
salt and pepper   to taste

GARNISH:
cherry tomatoes, sliced   7 oz (200 g)
 about 12
extra-virgin olive oil   1 tbsp (15 ml)
fresh parsley, minced   1 tsp (0.5 g)

Difficulty

Method

Heat the oil in a pan and cook the shallots until very tender. Add the mushrooms and the minced parsley. Lightly salt the vegetables and let them cook for a few minutes. Remove from the heat and add the bread and diced cheese. Grease individual ramekins and fill them with the mixture.

Beat the egg with the milk and grated Parmigiano. Season it with salt and pepper and pour it over the bread mixture. Bake it at 325° F (160° C) for about 20 minutes.

Rinse the tomatoes and slice them. Sauté the tomatoes in the oil and season with salt to taste. Top the bread pudding with tomatoes and minced parsley.

CACIOCAVALLO

In the realm of gastronomy, some of the greatest products are often given curious names of mysterious origin. Such is the case for caciocavallo – a semi-hard cheese shaped like a pear or flask, perhaps one of the oldest "stretchy" cheeses – which has been produced since at least the Middle Ages. According to some, the name comes from the tradition of tying two cheeses together and hanging them over a pole or beam to let them age, resulting in the expression cacio-a-cavallo, meaning "cheese on horseback." Others believe it comes from the herders' habit of tying pairs of cheeses to the horse's saddles when they came down from the mountain pastures. But the most likely explanation is perhaps the least bizarre: The name is from a stamp or seal depicting a horse which was placed on the cheese under the Kingdom of Naples. Whatever the story may be, this cheese has proven to be an Italian favorite for centuries.

EGGPLANT STUFFED WITH GOAT CHEESE

INVOLTINI DI MELANZANE AL CAPRINO

Preparation time: 35 minutes + 10 minutes cooking time

Ingredients for 4 servings

eggplant   1 3/4 lbs (800 g) about
   2 medium
**red onions, preferably Tropea, thinly
   sliced**   12 oz (350 g) about 2 small
tomatoes   14 oz (400 g) about 2 large
goat cheese   10 1/2 oz (300 g)
white vinegar   1 cup (250 ml)
sugar   2 tbsp + 2 tsp (30 g)
chives   1 bunch, sliced thin
basil leaves   6 large
extra-virgin olive oil   2/3 cup (150 ml)
salt and pepper   to taste

Method

Rinse the eggplant and slice them lengthwise in 1/4-inch thick slices. Sprinkle the eggplant slices generously with salt and let them drain for 20 minutes. Heat 6 tablespoons oil in a nonstick pan over medium heat and cook the eggplant until browned and tender on both sides. When they're done, lay them on paper towels to absorb the excess oil.

Mix the goat cheese with the chives and season with salt and pepper to taste. In a food processor, purée the tomatoes with about 2 tablespoons of olive oil. Strain the purée with a fine mesh strainer and season with salt and pepper. Slice the onions and heat them in a pan with the sugar and vinegar. When the liquid reaches a boil, turn off the heat and strain it. Purée the basil with 2 tablespoons of the olive oil.

Place a tablespoon of cheese in the middle of each eggplant slice and roll it up. Tie chive leaves around each eggplant rollup so it stays closed. Arrange them on serving plates with a spoonful of sweet and sour onions, a spoonful of tomato sauce and a drizzle of basil oil.

Difficulty

CARASAU FLATBREAD WITH VEGETABLES AND BUFFALO MOZZARELLA
CIALDE DI PANE CARASAU CON VERDURE E MOZZARELLA DI BUFALA

Preparation time: 30 minutes + 10 minutes cooking time

Ingredients for 4 servings

Carasau bread   4 slices
zucchini, sliced lengthwise, 1/4-inch thick
   10 1/2 oz (300 g)
eggplant, peeled and sliced   1 3/4 lbs
   (800 g)
ripe tomatoes, sliced 1/2-inch thick
   1 lb (450 g) about 3
buffalo mozzarella   1/2 lb (250 g)
basil, thinly sliced   to taste
extra-virgin olive oil   to taste
salt and pepper   to taste

Method

Clean the zucchini and slice it thinly lengthwise. Peel the eggplant and slice it into rounds, then sprinkle it with salt and place it in a strainer for at least 15 minutes to let any bitter liquid drain off.

In the meantime, grill the zucchini on a very hot grill until browned on both sides. Remove and set aside. When it's done, do the same with the eggplant, which should have drained and dried while the zucchini was cooking. Cut the tomatoes and mozzarella into slices of equal thickness.

Carasau bread is a flat bread from Sardinia. Break each piece of Carasau bread into 3 or 4 pieces and start arranging the ingredients on a serving plate. Start with a piece of bread, then add a slice of zucchini, followed by a slice of eggplant, a slice of tomato and a slice of mozzarella. Drizzle olive oil on top, then sprinkle on a pinch of salt and pepper and a bit of basil. Place another piece of bread on top. Repeat the process until all ingredients are used, which should result in 3 layers for each serving. Top each "tower" with a slice of tomato and mozzarella. Drizzle olive oil on top and sprinkle with basil.

Difficulty

FRIED STUFFED SQUASH BLOSSOMS

FIORI DI ZUCCA RIPIENI FRITTI

Preparation time: 40 minutes + 5-6 minutes cooking time

Ingredients for 4 servings

squash blossoms   12

zucchini, cut into small strips   6 1/3 oz (180 g) about 1 medium

anchovies packed in oil   1 oz (20 g)

extra-virgin olive oil   3 tbsp (40 ml) plus more for frying

warm water   1 tbsp (15 ml)

flour   1/3 cup + 1 tbsp (50 g)

FILLING:

ricotta cheese   10 1/2 oz (300 g)

Parmigiano-Reggiano cheese, grated 2/3 cup (60 g)

mint leaves, chopped   6

salt and pepper   to taste

BATTER:

cold water   3/4 cup + 2 tbsp + 2 tsp (200 ml)

all-purpose flour   1 2/3 cups (200 g)

egg   1

Method

Clean the squash blossoms and remove the pistils, being careful not to tear the petals. Combine the filling ingredients and mix them with a wooden spoon, seasoning with salt and pepper to taste. Use a pastry bag to fill the blossoms.

Cut the zucchini into small strips and sauté it with 1 tablespoon of oil, salt and pepper, until browned and tender.

Use an immersion blender to purée the anchovies, 2 tablespoon of oil and 1 tablespoon warm water. Strain the mixture to remove any bone remnants.

Quickly whisk together the batter ingredients in a large bowl. Lightly flour the blossoms, dip them in the batter and fry them a few at a time. Let the excess oil drip off, then lay them on paper towels. Sprinkle them with salt and transfer them to plates. Serve the fried squash blossoms with the zucchini, drizzling the anchovy dressing on top.

Difficulty

WARM SPELT SALAD WITH SHRIMP
INSALATINA TIEPIDA DI FARRO CON GAMBERI

Preparation time: 30 minutes + 10 minutes cooking time

Ingredients for 4 servings

spelt   3/4 cup (150 g)
shrimp   12
carrots, cut into fine dice   3 1/2 oz (100 g) about 2 small
zucchini, cut into fine dice   3 1/2 oz (100 g) about 1 small
tomato   3 1/2 oz (100 g) about 1 medium
peas   1/3 cup (50 g)
red onion, finely chopped   1 3/4 oz (50 g) about 1 small
minced parsley   1 tsp (0.5 g)
a few basil leaves, torn
extra-virgin olive oil   3 tbsp + 2 tsp (50 ml)
salt and pepper   to taste

Method

Bring a small saucepan of salted water to a boil. Add the peas and cook them until just tender. Drain and run the peas under cold water. Drain again. Heat 1 tablespoon + 2 teaspoons oil in a skillet over medium heat. Add the onion and cook until tender. Add the diced zucchini and carrots and season with salt and pepper. Cook until lightly browned but not softened.

Peel the tomato, remove the seeds and dice it. Boil the spelt in salted water, strain it and put it in a bowl. Add the cooked vegetables, diced tomatoes and basil. Season with cold-pressed olive oil and salt to taste.

Sauté the shrimp in a bit of oil until cooked through and browned. Serve them with the spelt salad.

Difficulty

MACKEREL SALAD
INSALATA DI SGOMBRO

Preparation time: 30 minutes + 30 minutes cooking time

Ingredients for 4 servings

fresh mackerel   32 oz (1 kg), about
  4 whole
mixed greens   6 oz (200 g)
**golden raisins, soaked in water and
  drained**   1/3 cup (50 g)
toasted pine nuts   1/4 cup + 2 tbsp (50 g)
green olives, chopped   1 3/4 oz (50 g)
  about 18
chives, chopped   1 tbsp (0.1 g)
mint leaves, chopped   1 tbsp (0.5 g)
extra-virgin olive oil   1/4 cup (60 ml)
balsamic vinegar   2 tsp (10 ml)
salt and pepper   to taste

COURT-BOUILLON:
water   8 1/2 cups (2 L)
vinegar   1 cup (250 ml)
carrots   2 4/5 oz (80 g) about 1 1/2 small
onions   5 1/3 oz (150 g) about 2 small
celery   2 1/2 oz (70 g) about 2 medium
  stalks
black peppercorns   5
bay leaf   1

Method

Make the *court-bouillon* first, putting all the ingredients in the water and letting it boil for 30 minutes. Soak the raisins in warm water for at least 15 minutes and drain.

Clean and gut the mackerel, rinsing them well under cold water.

Rinse the greens and chop up the olives.

Boil the mackerel in the *court-bouillon* for 10-12 minutes (cooking time will depend on the size of the fish), then let them cool. Fillet them and remove the bones, then divide each fillet into 4 pieces.

In a large bowl, mix together the greens, chives, and mint. Dress the mixture with the balsamic vinegar, salt and oil. Mix well and distribute it among serving plates, adding the olives, raisins and pine nuts. Add the mackerel fillets last. Drizzle olive oil on top and sprinkle with freshly ground pepper.

Difficulty

CAPONATA WITH MACKEREL
CAPONATA CON SGOMBRI

Preparation time: 10 minutes + 10 minutes cooking time

Ingredients for 4 servings

freselle (crisp round bread croutons) 4
cauliflower, trimmed and cut into
   florets 1 lb (500 g) about 1 large head
pickled mixed vegetables (Giardiniera
   or Jardinière) 5 1/3 oz (150 g)
pickled Neapolitan peppers 2
escarole, chopped 1 head
lettuce, chopped 1 head
capers 3 1/2 oz (100 g)
black olives 3 1/2 oz (100 g) about 20
salted anchovies 4
boiled or smoked mackerel 7 oz (200 g)
extra-virgin olive oil, plus more for
   serving 4 tbsp (60 ml)
white vinegar 3 1/2 oz (100 ml)
white wine 3 1/2 oz (100 ml)
lemon juice 1 tbsp (15 ml)
salt and ground pepper to taste

Method

Boil the cauliflower in water with salt and the lemon juice until tender. Combine it in a large salad bowl with the anchovies, pickled vegetables, pickled Neapolitan peppers, chopped escarole, lettuce, capers and olives. Season with a pinch of salt, pepper, a few tablespoons of oil and vinegar, and mix well.

In a container soak the "freselle" (crisp round bread croutons) in the remaining vinegar and wine; once softened, crumble rather roughly into the salad bowl and mix well.

On the top arrange the mackerel dressed with oil and lemon juice.

Difficulty

CITRUS-MARINATED ANCHOVIES WITH FENNEL SALAD

ALICI MARINATE AGLI AGRUMI CON INSALATA DI FINOCCHI

Preparation time: 30 minutes + 1 day to marinate

Ingredients for 4 servings

fresh anchovies   1.3 lbs (600 g)
fennel (about 3 bulbs), thinly sliced
  1.5 lbs (700 g)
orange   1
lemon   1
extra-virgin olive oil   3 1/2 tbsp (50 ml)
sprig of thyme   1
sprig of wild fennel   1
salt and pepper   to taste

Method

Clean the anchovies, removing the bones and innards. Peel the lemon and orange with a potato peeler, making sure you don't include any of the white part, and mince the peel. Juice the orange and lemon and set aside. Strip the thyme from the stem and roughly chop the wild fennel.

Arrange half the herbs in the bottom of a container. Add the minced citrus peel and a drizzle of extra-virgin olive oil. Place the anchovies on top. Cover them with the remaining herbs, the juice of the orange and lemon and a pinch of salt and pepper. Let the anchovies marinate for a full day in the refrigerator.

Wash and drain the fennel, cut into thin slices and arrange it on a platter. Top with the marinated anchovies and serve.

MARINATING

Food preparation doesn't necessarily mean cooking, even in the Italian tradition, and marinating is one example. A marinade is a sauce in which foods are left to soak for a long time, sometimes for a whole day. The presence of acidic ingredients (vinegar, citrus juices or alcoholic beverages) transforms the flavor, consistency and appearance of the food so that it's almost been "cold-cooked." This process is typical of Italian gastronomy, whether it's merely the preliminary phase of a more complicated recipe or simply a single food preparation step. It's a very ancient method that was created to extend the shelf life of food items, but it continues to be part of the Mediterranean tradition today because of its irrefutable value in terms of taste and nutrition.

Difficulty

FENNEL SALAD WITH SWORDFISH CARPACCIO
INSALATINA DI FINOCCHIO CON CARPACCIO DI SPADA

Preparation time: 20 minutes + 30 minutes to marinate

Ingredients for 4 servings

fennel, thinly sliced 1 1/2 bulbs lbs (350 g)
swordfish 14 oz (400 g)
juice of 2 lemons
wild fennel approx. 1/4 cup (20 g)
extra-virgin olive oil 1/4 cup (60 ml)
salt and pepper to taste

Method

Wash the fennel, slice it very thinly and put it in ice water.

Make a lemon dressing by whisking together 3 tablespoons of olive oil, the juice of half a lemon and salt and pepper to taste.

Strain and dry the fennel. Combine it with the lemon dressing and place it in the center of a serving plate. Arrange the swordfish slices around it (be sure to drain them well when removing them from the marinade). Drizzle with olive oil and garnish with fresh wild fennel and strips of lemon peel.

Skin the swordfish and slice it as thinly as possible with a very sharp knife. Arrange the slices in a shallow dish or tray and season them with salt and pepper to taste. Sprinkle them with wild fennel and drizzle lemon juice on top. Let them marinate for about 30 minutes in the refrigerator.

Difficulty

PASTA & SOUPS

CHAPTER TWO

SPAGHETTI WITH TOMATO SAUCE
SPAGHETTI AL POMODORO

Preparation time: 30 minutes + 8 minutes cooking time

Ingredients for 4 servings

spaghetti 12 oz (350 g)
extra-virgin olive oil 2 tbsp (30 ml)
peeled tomatoes or tomato purée
  1 1/3 lbs (600 g) about 2 1/2 cups
onion, chopped 2/3 cup (100 g)
garlic 1 clove
basil 8 leaves, chopped
Parmigiano-Reggiano cheese, grated
  1/4 cup (40 g)
salt and pepper to taste

Method

Sauté the chopped onion in the oil in a saucepan, together with the whole peeled clove of garlic. When the onion turns golden brown, add the chopped tomatoes, salt and pepper. Cook the sauce over high heat for about 20 minutes, stirring from time to time. When it is cooked, remove the garlic and add the washed, dried and roughly chopped basil.

Cook the spaghetti in salted boiling water until al dente; drain and add the tomato sauce. Sprinkle with the grated Parmigiano cheese.

"PUMMAROLA 'N COPPA" (TOMATOES ON TOP)

Enrico Caruso, the famous Neapolitan tenor, was an excellent cook and a great gourmet. And he had one gastronomic passion: spaghetti with tomato sauce.
During his New York years, he taught his American friends how to cook and serve this simple but sublime dish. Almost all the newspapers wrote about his culinary predilection and his laudable attempts to share it in a foreign land, to the point that, as the famous pianist Arthur Rubinstein recounted, every time Caruso went into a restaurant in New York and ordered a plate of spaghetti with tomato sauce, everybody stopped eating and stared at him. They wondered how he would eat: with his left or right hand? Using a spoon as well, or not? And would he twirl it round his fork? And what would he do with the spaghetti that was hanging down? Would he cut it with his knife or suck it up? Until one evening when the great singer was tired of being the center of attention. With a theatrical Neapolitan gesture, he threw his fork down in his plate, grabbed a handful of spaghetti and stuffed it into his mouth, splashing his face, tie, jacket and shirt with tomato sauce. And his audience was happy.

Difficulty

CAVATIELLI WITH TOMATOES AND RICOTTA
CAVATIELLI CON RICOTTA

Preparation time: 1 hour + 5-6 minutes cooking time

Ingredients for 4 servings

FOR THE PASTA:
semolina flour   1 3/4 cups (300 g)
water   2/3 cup (150 ml)

FOR THE SAUCE:
tomatoes   2.2 lbs (1 kg) about 6 large
aged ricotta cheese   5 1/3 oz (150 g)
extra-virgin olive oil   3 tbsp + 2 tsp
   (50 ml)
garlic clove   1
basil 1 bunch, torn   1
salt and pepper   to taste

Method

Let the water warm up to room temperature and mix it with the flour in a large bowl. When the dough is smooth and elastic, wrap it in plastic and refrigerate it for 15 minutes.

Shape the dough into long cylinders as thick as your finger and cut them into 1/2 inch (1 cm) pieces. Use a knife with a rounded tip to roll the pieces back and forth on the work surface, pressing down gently in the middle so the edges curl up.

Wash the tomatoes, remove the seeds, and dice them.

Heat the oil in a pan over medium heat. Add the whole garlic clove and be careful not to let it scorch. Add the tomatoes, season with a pinch of salt and pepper, and let it cook for 15 minutes. Then add the basil and let it cook for a few more minutes. Remember to remove the garlic clove at the end.

Meanwhile heat a large stockpot of water. When it reaches a boil, add a handful of coarse salt along with the cavatielli. Strain the pasta after 5-6 minutes and combine it with the tomato sauce. Sprinkle it with grated ricotta and drizzle cold-pressed olive oil on top.

Difficulty

CHEF'S TIPS

A traditional wooden cutting board is the ideal surface for making this kind of pasta. The dough won't slide around, making it easier to give the cavatielli their characteristic shape.

CELLENTANI WITH TOMATO PESTO

CELLENTANI AL PESTO DI POMODORO

Preparation time: 5 minutes + 10 minutes cooking time

Ingredients for 4 servings

cellentani pasta   10 1/2 oz (300 g)
large ripe tomatoes   about 5
Parmigiano-Reggiano cheese, grated
  2/3 cup (60 g)
pine nuts   2 tbsp (30 g)
peeled almonds   2 tbsp (30 g)
walnuts   2 tbsp (30 g)
extra-virgin olive oil   3 tbsp (45 ml)
mint leaves   5
garlic clove, peeled and minced   1
salt and pepper   to taste

Method

Using a knife, make an incision in the form of an X on the tomatoes and immerse them in a large pot of boiling water for 30-40 seconds. Using a slotted spoon, take the tomatoes out of the pot, saving the water for cooking the pasta.

Let the tomatoes cool in a bowl of cold water. Once cooled, peel them, divide into quarters, and remove the seeds.

To make the tomato pesto, place the tomatoes, pine nuts, peeled almonds, walnuts, garlic, mint leaves, grated Parmigano-Reggiano, and 2 tablespoons of the extra-virgin olive oil in a food processor. Pulse until the mixture is blended and smooth, then add salt and freshly ground pepper to taste.

Bring the water used for cooking the tomatoes to a boil once again, add a handful of coarse salt, and cook the cellentani pasta until al dente. Meanwhile, pour the pesto into a large bowl. Drain the pasta and combine with the pesto, adding a tablespoon of oil. Mix thoroughly. Serve on individual plates, topped with a drizzle of of oil, and if desired, another sprinkling of freshly ground black pepper. This pasta sauce can also be used with bavette pasta.

Difficulty

PENNE ALL'ARRABBIATA

PENNE ALL'ARRABBIATA

Preparation time: 30 minutes + 9 minutes cooking time

Ingredients for 4 servings

penne pasta   12 oz (350 g)
extra-virgin olive oil   2 tbsp (30 ml)
**crushed tomatoes or whole peeled
  tomatoes**   21 oz (600 g)
hot red pepper   to taste
garlic cloves, peeled and sliced   2
salt   to taste

Method

Sauté the garlic with the olive oil and hot red pepper to taste, but don't let it brown too much. If you're using fresh hot pepper it should be sliced, but if you're using dried hot pepper wear disposable gloves and crush it by hand.

Once the garlic and hot pepper are slightly browned, add the crushed tomatoes (or whole peeled tomatoes, chopped). Season with salt to taste and cook on high heat for 15 minutes, stirring occasionally.

Meanwhile, boil the penne in salted water. When it's al dente, drain it and combine it with the sauce.

Difficulty

CHEF'S TIPS

Penne rigate is recommended for arrabbiata sauce because the ridges hold the sauce very nicely.

GARGANELLI WITH PROSCIUTTO, PEPPERS, AND PEAS

GARGANELLI DI SFOGLIA CON PROSCIUTTO, PEPERONI E PISELLI

Preparation time: 15 minutes + 5 minutes cooking time

Ingredients for 4 servings

garganelli di sfoglia pasta   12 oz (350 g)

prosciutto di Parma, in one slice about 1/8 inch (3 mm) thick   5 1/3 oz (150 g)

peas   about 2/3 cup (100 g)

red bell pepper, peeled, seeded, diced, and quartered   7 oz (200 g) about 1 large

heavy cream   3/4 cup + 2 tbsp (200 ml)

unsalted butter   2 tbsp (30 g)

Parmigiano-Reggiano cheese, grated 2/3 cup (60 g)

salt and pepper   to taste

Method

Melt the unsalted butter over low heat and add the prosciutto, diced very finely (about 1/8 inch or 3 mm). When it's browned, add the red pepper (roasted, peeled, and diced). After a few seconds add the cream. Let it simmer over low heat until the sauce reaches a boil. Remove it from the heat, season with salt and pepper to taste, and keep it warm.

Boil the garganelli in salted water and add the peas for the last 3-5 minutes, letting them cook together. Strain them both when the pasta is al dente. Combine the pasta and peas with the sauce and stir in the grated Parmigiano. Serve immediately.

Difficulty

CHEF'S TIPS

A tasty alternative is to substitute sausage, cut into 1/3-3/4 inch (1-2 cm) pieces, for the prosciutto. If you can't find garganelli, penne pasta is a good substitute aswell.

PENNETTE WITH ROASTED BELL PEPPERS, CHICKEN, AND ANCHOVIES

PENNETTE CON PEPERONI ARROSTITI, POLLO E ACCIUGHE

Preparation time: 40 minutes + 10 minutes cooking time

Ingredients for 4 servings

pennette rigate pasta   12 oz (350 g)
red bell pepper   7 oz (200 g) about 1 large
yellow bell pepper   7 oz (200 g) about
   1 large
chicken breast   10 1/2 oz (300 g)
anchovy fillets   1 3/4 oz (50 g)
dry white wine   4 tbsp (50 ml)
extra-virgin olive oil   3 tbsp (40 ml)
basil leaves   3
garlic clove   1
salt and pepper   to taste

Method

Arrange the peppers in a pan and roast them in the oven at 350° F (180° C) for 15 minutes. When they're tender, put them in a container and seal it well with plastic wrap (make sure it's airtight) so they'll be easier to peel. In the meantime, dice the chicken breast. Then peel the peppers, remove the seeds, and cut them into thin strips.

Brown the chicken with the oil and the whole garlic clove. After a few minutes add the anchovies, basil (cut into strips), and white wine. Let all the liquid evaporate. Add the peppers, season with salt and pepper to taste, and let it all simmer for a minute. Remove the garlic clove.

Boil the pasta in salted water until al dente. Combine it with the sauce and mix well.

CHEF'S TIPS

You can also roast the peppers over the burner on a gas stove, holding them with a large fork and letting them blister over the flame. Placing the roasted peppers in an airtight container makes the cleaning process quicker and easier, because the condensation produced by the high temperature of the pepper helps detach the skin.

Difficulty

LIGURIAN PASTA WITH PESTO
TROFIE AL PESTO

Preparation time: 30 minutes + 30 minutes resting time + 5 minutes cooking time

Ingredients for 4 servings

FOR THE PASTA:
"0" type flour   2 1/2 cups (300 g)
water   2/3 cup (150 ml)
or: **ready made trofie**   14 oz (400 g)

FOR THE SAUCE:
basil   1 oz (30 g)
pine nuts   about 2 tbsp (15 g)
Parmigiano-Reggiano cheese, grated
  2 oz (60 g)
Aged Pecorino cheese, grated   1 1/3 oz
  (40 g)
garlic   1 clove
green beans   3 1/2 oz (100 g) about 18
  beans, cut into 1/4 inch pieces
potatoes, peeled and diced   7 oz (200 g)
  about 1 1/2 medium
extra-virgin olive oil, preferably
  Ligurian   3/4 cup + 2 tbsp (200 ml)
salt   to taste

Difficulty

Method

Mound the flour on a work surface, make a well in the center and knead with sufficient water to make a firm, elastic dough. Cover the dough with plastic wrap and let it rest for 30 minutes before using.

To make the trofie, break off small pieces the size of chickpeas and roll them in your hands (or roll them on the work surface, pressing down lightly at the same time) to make a slender corkscrew shape. Alternatively, buy ready-made trofie.

Prepare and wash the basil, then dry it in a cloth. Crush the basil, pine nuts and the peeled clove of garlic with 3/4 cup olive oil, a pinch of salt and the grated cheese in a mortar. Alternatively, blend the ingredients in a food processor, using the pulse function so the pesto does not overheat. When the ingredients are well mixed, pour them into a bowl and cover with the rest of the extra-virgin olive oil.

Boil the diced potatoes and the green beans in a large saucepan. When the vegetables are almost cooked, add the trofie to the same pan and cook until the pasta is al dente. Remove from the heat and drain, reserving a little of the water. Add the pesto and stir well, diluting with a little cooking water and a little extra-virgin olive oil.

A LIGURIAN WEDDING

Trofie are small gnocchi made with water and flour in a long slender curled corkscrew shape. They are typical of Ligurian cuisine, or Genoese cuisine to be more precise (trofie means gnocchi in Genoese dialect). The dough can be made with white or whole wheat flour to make dark-colored trofie, or chestnut flour for pasta with a sweeter flavor. Traditionally trofie are boiled together with potatoes and green beans and then mixed with the tasty and aromatic basil pesto that is also typical of Liguria.

CUT SPAGHETTI WITH BROCCOLI
SPAGHETTI TAGLIATI CON BROCCOLI

Preparation time: 40 minutes + 6 minutes cooking time

Ingredients for 4 servings

cut spaghetti   12 oz (350 g)
broccoli   1 lb (500 g)
prosciutto (dry-cured), in one slice
  2 oz (60 g)
pork rinds   2 oz (60 g)
extra-virgin olive oil   1 tbsp + 2 tsp
  (20 ml)
yellow onions sliced   3 1/2 oz (100 g)
  about 1 1/2 small
garlic clove   1
**Pecorino cheese, grated (preferably
  Romano)**   1/2 cup + 2 tbsp (60 g)
water   4 1/4 cups (1 L)
salt and pepper   to taste

Method

Divide the broccoli into florets, wash it thoroughly, and cook it in lightly salted water on medium heat. When it's done, remove the pot from the heat.

Slice the onion, crush the garlic, and cut the prosciutto into small strips. Sauté the onion and garlic in the oil until they turn golden brown, then add the prosciutto to the pot. Mix well and add the water.

Meanwhile clean the pork rinds very carefully, removing any bristles. Slice the rinds thinly. Blanch them in unsalted water, then add them to the pot with the prosciutto and water. Bring it to a boil, add a pinch of salt and pepper, and let it cook for about 5 minutes. Add the spaghetti and let it cook in the soup. A few minutes before you turn off the heat, add the broccoli florets with some of the water they cooked in (the soup should be slightly dense).

Serve with grated cheese and a generous sprinkling of pepper.

Difficulty

FETTUCCINE IN VEGETABLE RAGÙ
FETTUCCINE AL RAGÙ DI VERDURE

Preparation time: 40 minutes + 4-6 minutes cooking time

Ingredients for 4 servings

PASTA:

soft wheat flour (preferably Italian-type flour)   2 cups + 3 tbsp (300 g)
eggs   3
or: **ready made fettuccine** 1 lb (450 g)

SAUCE:

tomatoes, peeled, seeded and diced   5 1/3 oz (150 g) about 1 1/2 small
leek   about 1 small
eggplant, diced   2/3 cup (50 g)
zucchini, diced   1/2 small (50 g)
red bell pepper, diced   1 3/4 oz (50 g) about 1/2 small
yellow bell pepper, diced   1 3/4 oz (50 g) about 1/2 small
carrots, diced   1 3/4 oz (50 g) about 1 small
celery, diced   1 3/4 oz (50 g) about 3 small stalks
peas   1/4 cup (25 g)
basil leaves, roughly chopped   6
extra-virgin olive oil   3 tbsp + 2 tsp (50 ml)
salt   to taste

Difficulty

Method

Make a well with flour on a work surface. Add the eggs to the center of the well and gradually incorporate the flour. Knead the dough until it is smooth and elastic. Wrap it in plastic and refrigerate for 30 minutes. Use a rolling pin or pasta machine to roll out sheets of dough just under 1/16 inches. (1.5 mm) thick. Cut the dough into 1/4-inch (6 mm) wide strips.

Meanwhile, clean all of the vegetables. Dice the eggplant, sprinkle it with salt and let the liquid drain off. Dice the carrot, celery, peppers and zucchini. Boil the peas in lightly salted water until tender. Drain, rinse with cold water, and drain again.

Slice the white part of the leek into rounds and sauté it in the oil until tender. Add the red and yellow peppers and cook until tender. Add the zucchini , the eggplant, the carrots, celery and peas and cook until tender. Season with salt to taste. Add the tomato (peeled and diced, with seeds removed) and let everything cook for a few more minutes until the flavors meld together. Finish with the roughly chopped basil.

Boil the pasta in salted water, drain it, and toss with the vegetable ragù. Sprinkle ground pepper on top and serve.

WHOLE WHEAT SPAGHETTI WITH CREAMY ASPARAGUS AND GOAT CHEESE

SPAGHETTI INTEGRALI CON CREMA DI ASPARAGI E CAPRINO

Preparation time: 30 minutes + 8 minutes cooking time

Ingredients for 4 servings

whole wheat spaghetti   12 oz (350 g)
asparagus   14 oz (400 g)
fresh goat cheese   2 4/5 oz (80 g)
fresh basil   1 bunch leaves torn
shallot   1
fresh mint   5 leaves, torn
garlic clove   1/2
extra-virgin olive oil   2 tbsp (30 ml)
salt and pepper   to taste

Method

Clean and rinse the asparagus. Remove the tougher parts of the stems and slice them into rounds. Keep the tips separate and boil them in salted water. Set aside 1/4 cup + 1 tablespoon of the water after straining them.

Mince the shallot and sauté it in the oil with the half garlic clove. When they've turned golden brown, add the sliced asparagus stems and season with salt and pepper. Then add a few hand-torn mint and basil leaves. Add the reserved water and let cook for 10 minutes, then purée everything.

Boil the spaghetti in salted water until al dente. Combine with the purée and asparagus tips, and let it all cook together for a minute. Distribute it among the serving plates and top each one with a quenelle (spoonful) of fresh goat cheese.

Difficulty

RUOTE WITH BELL PEPPERS

RUOTE AI PEPERONI

Preparation time: 20 minutes + 8 minutes cooking time

Ingredients for 4 servings

ruote pasta   12 oz (350 g)

extra-virgin olive oil   3 tbsp + 2 tsp (50 ml)

red bell pepper, sliced into thin strips   4 1/2 lb (130 g) about 1 medium

yellow bell pepper, sliced into thin strips   4 1/2 lb (130 g) about 1 medium

onion   3 1/2 oz (100 g) about 1 1/2 small

heavy cream   1/3 cup + 1 1/2 tbsp (100 ml)

vegetable broth   as needed (best if fresh)

salt and pepper   to taste

FOR THE VEGETABLE BROTH:

carrot   half

celery stalk, with a few leaves   half

onion   half

water   4 1/4 cups (1 L)

salt   to taste

Method

Start by making the vegetable broth. Wash and peel half a carrot, half an onion, and half a celery stalk with a few leaves still attached. Boil them for at least 30 minutes in 4 1/4 cups (1 L) of water, seasoning with salt to taste. When the broth is done, strain it and use it for the pasta sauce.

Slice the onion and sauté it in the oil. When the onion is golden brown, add the peppers (cleaned and cut into thin strips).

Let the vegetables cook, adding vegetable broth as necessary. Continue until the peppers are soft, seasoning with salt and pepper to taste. When they're done, stir in the cream.

Boil the pasta in salted water until it's al dente, and combine it with the pepper sauce.

Difficulty

PENNE WITH ASPARAGUS
PENNE AGLI ASPARAGI

Preparation time: 15 minutes + 11 minutes cooking time

Ingredients for 4 servings

penne rigate pasta   12 oz (350 g)
asparagus   1/2 lb (250 g)
unsalted butter   3 tbsp + 2 tsp (50 g)
Parmigiano-Reggiano cheese, grated
  1/3 cup + 1 tbsp (40 g)
garlic cloves   2
eggs   2
fresh red hot pepper   to taste
salt   to taste

Method

Carefully wash the asparagus and remove the tough parts. Slice the stems into rounds and leave the tips whole. Put them in a pot (terracotta if possible) with the unsalted butter, the two garlic cloves and a bit of hot pepper (at your discretion). Stew them for about 10 minutes on medium heat.

Beat the eggs in a bowl with the grated Parmigiano and a pinch of salt.

Boil the pasta in salted water until it's al dente. Remove the garlic from the pot of asparagus, and add the pasta. Then add the egg and cheese mixture, quickly stir it into the pasta, and serve immediately.

Difficulty

CAVATELLI WITH ARUGULA AND POTATOES

CAVATELLI, RUGHETTA E PATATE

Preparation time: 20 minutes + 30 minutes cooking time

Ingredients for 4 servings

cavatelli pasta   14 oz (400 g)
arugula   5 1/3 oz (150 g)
**canned whole plum tomatoes
  crushed by hand**   5 1/3 oz (150 g)
potatoes, peeled and diced   5 1/3 oz
  (150 g)
extra-virgin olive oil   2 tbsp (30 ml)
garlic, 1 clove, sliced
basil leaves   4
salt and pepper   to taste

Method

Sauté sliced garlic in a couple of tablespoons of oil; add the basil and tomatoes and a pinch of salt, then cook over low heat until the sauce has thickened.

Meanwhile, bring salted water to a boil in a large pot and boil the peeled and diced (about 1 inch/3 cm cubes) potatoes. When almost done, add some arugula, and, once the water is boiling again, the cavatelli. Once cooked, drain, put everything back into the pot then add the tomato sauce. Top with a little arugula and serve hot.

Difficulty

ORECCHIETTE WITH BROCCOLI RABE

ORECCHIETTE CON CIME DI RAPA

Preparation time: 30 minutes + 15 minutes resting time + 5 minutes cooking time

Ingredients for 4 servings

FOR THE PASTA:

remilled durum wheat semolina flour
  1 1/3 cups (250 g)
water, lukewarm   1/2 cup (125 ml)
or: **ready made orecchiette**

FOR THE SAUCE:

rapini or broccoli rabe (cime di rapa)
  10 1/2 oz (300 g), trimmed
anchovies in oil   2 fillets
sliced fresh chili pepper   1
garlic   1 clove
extra-virgin olive oil   1/4 cup (60 ml)
freshly ground pepper   to taste
salt   to taste

Method

Make a well with the flour, add the lukewarm water to the well and knead to make smooth homogeneous dough. Wrap the dough in plastic and let it rest for at least 15 minutes.

Divide the dough into ropes about the thickness of a finger. Cut the ropes into small pieces about 1/2 inch (1 cm) long, with a round ended knife, and gently press flat on a work surface. Take each piece of dough in the palm of your hand and press with the thumb of your other hand to shape the orecchiette (little ears).

Trim the broccoli rabe, removing almost all of the tougher parts of the stem. In a wide, shallow skillet, fry a mixture of finely sliced garlic, the whole chili pepper and the two anchovy filets in 3 tablespoons of oil. Then add 3 or 4 tablespoons of water. When the anchovies have melted, remove the skillet from the heat.

Meanwhile, heat the water for the orecchiette in a large saucepan. When it boils, add a handful of coarse salt and pour in the pasta together with the broccoli rabe. Cook the pasta until al dente. A couple of minutes before draining the pasta, reheat the anchovy mixture.

Drain the orecchiette, preferably with a fine sieve, in order to catch all the small pieces of broccoli rabe, then add them directly to the fried anchovy mixture and mix well. Season with freshly ground pepper and serve immediately.

Difficulty

RICOTTA GNOCCHI WITH ARUGULA PESTO

GNOCCHI DI RICOTTA AL PESTO DI RUCOLA

Preparation time: 40 minutes + 2 minutes cooking time

Ingredients for 4 servings

FOR THE GNOCCHI:

fresh ricotta   14 oz (400 g)

soft wheat flour (preferably Italian-type flour)   about 1 cup (120 g)

Parmigiano-Reggiano cheese, grated   1/3 cup + 1 tbsp (40 g)

egg   1

nutmeg   to taste

salt and pepper   to taste

FOR THE PESTO:

arugula   4 1/5 oz (120 g) about 6 cups

tomatoes, very ripe   2 small

almonds   1/3 oz (10 g) about 8-9

Parmigiano-Reggiano cheese, grated   1/4 cup (25 g)

extra-virgin olive oil   1/4 cup + 1 tbsp (70 ml)

garlic clove   1/2

salt and pepper   to taste

Method

Put the ricotta into a large bowl. Mix it with the flour, egg, and Parmigiano. Season with salt, pepper and ground nutmeg. Transfer the resulting dough to a work surface and roll it out to a thickness of 1/2 inch (1 cm). Cut it into small diamonds.

Wash the arugula and combine it with the other ingredients in a food processor. Pulse until the mixture is homogenous and has reached a smooth consistency.

Wash the tomatoes and cut an X into the bottom of each one. Boil them for about 10 seconds, then submerge them in ice water. Peel them, remove the seeds and liquid, and dice them. Combine them with the pesto in a bowl.

Boil the gnocchi in salted water and skim them out as soon as they float to the surface. Combine them with the pesto and tomatoes. Mix well and serve, garnishing with fried arugula leaves to taste.

Difficulty

SPINACH GNOCCHI WITH PARMIGIANO-REGGIANO

GNOCCHI DI SPINACI AL PARMIGIANO-REGGIANO

Preparation time: 25 minutes + 5 minutes cooking time

Ingredients for 4 servings

spinach cooked and squeezed dry
  1 2/3 cups cooked (300 g)
ricotta cheese   10 1/2 oz (300 g)
Parmigiano-Reggiano cheese, grated
  1 1/2 cups (150 g)
**soft wheat flour (preferably Italian-
  type flour)**   1 cup + 3 tbsp (150 g)
eggs   2
unsalted butter   5 1/2 tbsp (80 g)
nutmeg   to taste
salt   to taste

Method

Pass the spinach through a vegetable mill, then combine it with the ricotta, eggs, flour, 1 cup of Parmigiano, and a pinch of salt and nutmeg. Mix it all together very thoroughly it forms a thick, consistent dough.

Form long cylinders about 1/2- to 2/3-inch (1.5-cm) thick, then cut them crosswise into 3/4-inch (2-cm) gnocchi and boil them in salted water for a few minutes. Strain the gnocchi and mix them with the melted unsalted butter and the remaining Parmigiano. As an alternative, they could also be served with tomato sauce or meat sauce.

Difficulty

HERBED RICOTTA GNOCCHI
PERLE DI RICOTTA ED ERBE

Preparation time: 30 minutes + 3-4 minutes cooking time

Ingredients for 4 servings

FOR THE GNOCCHI:
fresh ricotta   1 lbs (500 g)
flour   1 cup (125 g)
Parmigiano-Reggiano cheese   1 cup
  (100 g)
egg   1
**fresh herbs, finely chopped and mixed
  (parsley, thyme, sage, chives, and fresh
  oregano)**   2 4/5 oz (80 g) about 1 1/2
  cups

FOR THE TOPPING:
zucchini   1/2 lb (250 g) about 2 small
squash blossoms   3 1/2 oz (100 g)
  about 12
spring onions   4
small truffle   1
fresh mint   2-3 leaves, chopped
unsalted butter   3 tbsp + 2 tsp (50 g)
extra-virgin olive oil   3 tbsp + 2 tsp
  (50 ml)
salt and pepper   to taste

Method

Put the ricotta into a large mixing bowl. Add all the other gnocchi ingredients and mix well. Form tiny balls, about 3/4 inch (2 cm) in diameter.

Wash and dice the zucchini, and mince the spring onions.

Heat the oil and unsalted butter in a pan and sauté the spring onions. Add the zucchini and cook on high heat for a few more minutes. Wash and julienne the squash blossoms, and add them to the pan. When it's all cooked, purée 1/3 of the mixture. Add the purée back to the rest of the sauce, season with salt and pepper and add the chopped fresh mint leaves.

Boil the gnocchi in salted water. Once they begin floating to the surface, let them cook for 1 more minute then skim off and place them directly into the pan with the sauce. Stir to combine and top each serving with grated truffle.

Difficulty

BAVETTE PASTA WITH SWORDFISH AND CHERRY TOMATOES
BAVETTE CON PESCE SPADA E POMODORINI

Preparation time: 20 minutes + 10 minutes cooking time

Ingredients for 4 servings

bavette pasta (or substitute spaghetti)
   10 1/2 oz (300 g)
swordfish, cut into 1/2- inch cubes
   10 1/2 oz (300 g)
cherry tomatoes, halved   10 1/2 oz (300
   g) about 18
extra-virgin olive oil   3 tbsp (40 ml)
garlic clove   1
wild fennel (fennel pollen)   to taste
salt, pepper and hot red pepper   to taste

Method

Heat 1 tablespoon + 2 teaspoon oil in a nonstick pan and sear the swordfish until browned. Season it with salt, pepper and wild fennel to taste.

Separately, sauté the whole garlic clove and hot red pepper in the remaining oil. Slice the tomatoes in half and add them. Season with salt to taste and let cook for a few minutes. Finally, add the fish.

Boil the pasta in salted water and strain it when it's al dente. Add it to the pan with the sauce and let everything cook together for a few seconds, mixing well, and serve.

SWORDFISH

Catching swordfish is a centuries-old ritual steeped in tradition. It's a bona fide battle between fish and man, the latter armed with harpoons and out to capture one of the princes of the Mediterranean (Mediterranean swordfish reach a maximum length of 10 ft/3m and weigh up to 772 lbs/350 kg). During their mating season which is between June and August in the Mediterranean, swordfish begin a long migration toward the shore. This is when the fishermen take to the sea in specifically designed boats, ready for the hunt. A lookout, positioned in the crow's nest, alerts the rest to any swordfish sightings. According to legend, the sound of the Italian language was said to scare off the fish, so Sicilian and Calabrian fisherman spoke only Greek while out at sea, using common, standardized phrases. Not only were they sure this language wouldn't scare the fish, they believed that the ancient sounds would actually attract the fish, almost magically.

Difficulty

BUCATINI WITH CUTTLEFISH AND PEAS

BUCATINI CON SEPPIE E PISELLI

Preparation time: 30 minutes + 12 minutes cooking time

Ingredients for 4 servings

bucatini pasta   12 oz (350 g)
cuttlefish   12 oz (350 g)
peas, fresh or frozen   about 1 1/3 cup
  (200 g)
tomatoes, crushed   5 1/3 oz (150 g)
onion   1 small
garlic   1 clove
fresh basil   5-6 leaves
dry white wine   1/3 cup + 2 tbsp (1 dl)
extra-virgin olive oil   3 tbsp + 2 tsp
  (50 ml)
salt and pepper   to taste

Method

Peel and chop the onion and garlic. Clean and rinse the cuttlefish, then cut it into thin strips or very fine fillets, about 1/16-1/8 inch (2-3 mm) thick.

Drizzle a bit of olive oil in a pan and start browning the onion and garlic. Add the cuttlefish and cook for a few minutes, stirring continuously. Add the white wine; when it has evaporated add the crushed tomatoes, peas, and basil leaves. Cook for another 15 minutes.

Meanwhile boil the pasta in salted water. When it's al dente, strain it well and transfer it to a large bowl. Toss the pasta with the cuttlefish sauce and serve hot.

Difficulty

CHEF'S TIPS

The faster the cuttlefish cooks, the more tender it will be. As cuttlefish is a close relative of squid; although the flavors are not the same, you could substitute small squid if you can't find cuttlefish.
If you want the peas to have a vivid green color, you can blanch them separately. Boil them in lightly salted water for 3-4 minutes, then strain them and immediately put them in ice water to cool. Only add them to the cuttlefish for the last few minutes of cooking.

TROFIE PASTA AND CLAMS IN PESTO SAUCE

TROFIE AL PESTO E VONGOLE

Preparation time: 1 hour + 5 minutes cooking time

Ingredients for 4 servings

all-purpose flour   2 1/2 cups (300 g)
water   2/3 cup (150 ml)
clams   about 2 lbs (1 kg)
fresh basil leaves   1 1/4 cups (30 g)
pine nuts   2 tbsp (15 g)
Parmigiano-Reggiano cheese, grated
   2/3 cup (60 g)
aged Pecorino cheese, grated   1/3 cup +
   1 tbsp (40 g)
garlic clove   1
green beans   3 1/2 oz (100 g) about 18
   beans, cut into 1/4 inch pieces
potatoes, 7 oz, cut into fine dice
   1 1/2 small (200 g)
extra-virgin olive oil, preferably Ligurian
   3/4 cup + 1 1/2 tbsp (200 ml)
salt   to taste

Method

Pour the flour onto a work surface and create a well in the center. Add the water a little at a time and mix until the dough is relatively dense and elastic. Wrap it in plastic and let it sit for 30 minutes before working with it further.

Flush any sand out of the clams and rinse them well in cold water. Put them in a covered pot over high heat (with no liquid except for the water that remains on them after rinsing) and let them cook until they open, then remove clams from the shells.

Pinch off pieces of dough the size of a chickpea and roll them into thin strips between your hands (or roll them on a work surface, exerting slight pressure with your palm) to make the trofie.

Rinse the basil and towel dry. Crush the basil in a mortar with the pine nuts, garlic, a pinch of salt and the grated cheeses, adding just enough oil to make the mixture creamy. You can also do this in a food processor, using the pulse setting so the pesto doesn't overheat. Pour it all into a bowl and cover it with a layer of extra-virgin olive oil.

Boil the potatoes in salted water until just tender. Add the green beans and the pasta to the pot and cook until the pasta is al dente and the green beans are crisp-tender. Strain everything and add it to the pot of clams. Let it all cook together for a minute, then remove it from the heat. Combine it with the pesto and mix well, adding a bit of pasta water and olive oil.

Difficulty

SEDANINI WITH ARUGULA PESTO AND SALMON

SEDANINI CON PESTO DI RUCOLA E SALMONE

Preparation time: 35 minutes + 12 minutes cooking time

Ingredients for 4 servings

sedanini rigati pasta   12 oz (350 g)
arugula   3 1/2 oz (100 g) about 5 cups
extra-virgin olive oil   3/4 cup +
   1 1/2 tbsp (200 ml)
garlic   1 clove
pine nuts   about 2 1/2 tbsp (20 g)
potato   1 3/4 oz (50 g) about 1 small
vegetable broth (fresh or bouillon cube)
   3 tbsp + 2 tsp (50 ml)
salt and pepper   to taste
salmon   7 oz (200 g)
shallot, minced   2 tbsp (20 g)
fresh rosemary, minced   1 tsp (0.7 g)
cherry tomatoes, quartered   4 1/5 oz
   (120 g) about 7
vodka   1 tsp (5 ml)

Method

Boil the potatoes in salted water until tender. Strain them and purée them with the arugula, garlic, pine nuts, vegetable broth, and 2/3 cup (150 ml) of olive oil.

Sauté the shallot in the remaining oil. Slice the salmon into thin strips and add it to the shallot. Add the vodka and let it evaporate over high heat. Add the tomatoes (cut into quarters) and the minced rosemary. Let the mixture cook for 4-5 minutes, then combine with the arugula pesto.

Boil the pasta in salted water and strain it when it's al dente. Combine it with the sauce and mix well. Another option is to add the cooked pasta to the pan with the salmon and let them cook together for a minute, then spread some arugula pesto on each plate and place a portion of pasta on top.

Difficulty

BAVETTE WITH SHRIMP, MARSALA, AND FRESH SPRING ONIONS

BAVETTE CON GAMBERONI, MARSALA E CIPOLLOTTI FRESCHI

Preparation time: 1 hour + 8 minutes cooking time

Ingredients for 4 servings

bavette or fettucine pasta   12 oz (350 g)
jumbo shrimp, shell-on   14 oz (400 g)
celery, chopped   2/3 cup (70 g)
carrots, chopped   2/3 cup (80 g)
onion, chopped   2/3 cup (100 g)
spring onion, finely chopped   1 cup (100 g)
tomato paste   about 1 1/2 tbsp (25 g)
garlic   2 cloves
dry Marsala wine   3/4 cup + 2 tbsp
   (200 ml)
extra-virgin olive oil   1/4 cup (60 ml)
salt and pepper   to taste

Method

Clean and shell the shrimp and cut them into small pieces.

Chop the celery, carrots, and onion. Sauté them in a saucepan with half the oil and the 2 whole garlic cloves. After 5 minutes, add the shrimp shells and let them brown thoroughly. Then add the tomato paste and Marsala. Let all the liquid evaporate, then pour in 4 1/4 cups (1 L) of water. Let the sauce simmer for 30 minutes and season with salt and pepper. Filter the sauce when it's done.

Finely chop the spring onion and sauté it in the rest of the oil. Add the shrimp and season with salt and pepper. Slowly add the filtered sauce and let it cook for a few minutes.

Boil the pasta in salted water until al dente. Add it to the shrimp sauce and cook it all together for a minute, stirring well to combine.

CHEF'S TIPS

For a more intense flavor, you can use the shrimp heads in the sauce. Just crush them with a meat pounder and add them along with the shells. The same technique can be used for other crustaceans, like lobster or scampi.

Difficulty

LINGUINE WITH BROAD BEANS, OLIVES AND HAKE
LINGUINE CON NASELLO, FAVE E OLIVE

Preparation time: 50 minutes + 8 minutes cooking time

Ingredients for 4 servings

linguine   12 oz (350 g)
broad beans, fresh (fava beans)   1 1/3 cups (200 g)
hake fillets, cut into 1/4-inch dice   1/2 lb (250 g)
black olives, pitted and chopped   1 3/4 oz (50 g) about 12 large
onion, finely chopped   1 oz (30 g) about 1/2 small
garlic   1 clove
parsley, minced   1 tbsp (0.5 g)
extra-virgin olive oil   3 tbsp (40 ml)
salt and pepper   to taste

VEGETABLE BROTH:
water   2 cups (500 ml)
onion   2 3/5 oz (75 g) about 1 small
carrot   1 1/3 oz (40 g) about 1 small
celery   1 medium stalk (30 g)

Method

Make the broth by adding the onion, carrot, and celery to the cold water. Let the water boil for about 30 minutes, then strain it and set it aside.

Finely chop the onion and sauté it in the oil with the whole, peeled garlic clove. When the onion and garlic turn golden brown, add the chopped hake and season with salt and pepper. Add the shelled fava beans to the sauce. Add enough broth to cover everything and cook until the favas are tender and the fish is cooked through, about 10 minutes. Stir in the olives.

In a large saucepan filled with boiling, salted water cook the pasta until it is al dente. Drain the pasta and transfer it to the pan with the sauce. Let everything cook together for a minute, mixing well.

Sprinkle minced parsley and freshly ground pepper over each serving and drizzle cold-pressed olive oil on top.

Difficulty

STROZZAPRETI WITH SCALLOPS AND PESTO

STROZZAPRETI CON CAPESANTE E PESTO

Preparation time: 40 minutes + 10 minutes cooking time

Ingredients for 4 servings

strozzapreti pasta   12 oz (350 g)
scallops   4 large
extra-virgin olive oil   1 tbsp + 2 tsp (20 ml)
parsley, minced   1 tbsp (0.5 g)

FOR THE FISH SAUCE:

white fish (hake)   3 1/2 oz (100 g)
carrots   2 4/5 oz (80 g) about 1 1/2 small
celery stalks   2 1/2 oz (70 g) about
  2 medium
onions   5 1/3 oz (150 g) about 2 small
flour   4 tbsp (30 g)
unsalted butter   2 tbsp (30 g)
water   4 1/4 cups (1 L)
salt and pepper   to taste

FOR THE PESTO:

fresh basil leaves   about 1 1/4 cups
  (30 g)
Parmigiano-Reggiano cheese, grated
  2/3 cup (60 g)
aged Pecorino cheese, grated   1/3 cup
  + 1 tbsp (40 g)
pine nuts   about 1 tbsp (10 g)
extra-virgin olive oil   3/4 cup + 2 tbsp
  (200 ml)
garlic   1 clove
salt   to taste

Difficulty

Method

Blend the basil, pine nuts, peeled garlic, and oil in a food processor. Then add the two grated cheeses and mix well. Season the pesto with salt to taste and refrigerate it.

Boil the vegetables and fish in 1 1/4 cups of water for at least 20 minutes. When the broth is done, strain it and set it aside for later use.

Start the cream sauce by melting the unsalted butter in a pot. Add the flour, whisking continuously, and let it cook for 1-2 minutes. Season with salt and pepper, then add 2 cups (500 ml) of fish broth. Let it cook until the sauce is smooth and creamy.

Clean and cube the scallops, and sauté them in the oil. Boil the pasta in salted water and strain it a few minutes earlier than the time indicated on the package instructions. Combine it with the pesto, scallops, and a few ladlefuls of cream sauce.

Transfer the pasta to a greased baking dish and bake it at 350° F (180° C) for 10 minutes. Sprinkle with minced parsley and serve.

ORECCHIETTE PASTA WITH UMBRINE, MUSSELS AND BROCCOLI

ORECCHIETTE CON OMBRINA, COZZE E BROCCOLI

Preparation time: 1 hour + 8-9 minutes cooking time

Ingredients for 4 servings

PASTA:

durum wheat semolina   1 3/4 cups (300 g)
water   2/3 cup (150 ml)

SAUCE:

umbrine or substitute sea bass or branzino   7 oz (200 g)
tomatoes   1/2 lbs (250 g)
mussels, scrubbed and de-bearded   10 1/2 oz (300 g)
broccoli, cut into florets   7 oz (200 g)
white wine   3 tbsp + 2 tsp (50 ml)
fresh marjoram, minced   1 tsp
extra-virgin olive oil   1/4 cup (60 ml) + extra for serving
salt and pepper   to taste

Method

Mix the flour and hot water until a smooth and elastic dough forms. Wrap it in plastic and refrigerate it for 15 minutes.

Shape the dough into cylinders as thick as your finger and cut them crosswise into pieces about 1/3-1/2 inch (1 cm) long. Use the rounded tip of a butter knife to slide them over the work surface. Then use your thumb to form a depression in the center of each one, creating the typical concave orecchiette shape.

Clean the mussels thoroughly, scraping them with a knife and rinsing them well. Put them in a pot with the white wine and 1 tablespoon of oil. Cover the pot and let them cook until they open, then remove half the shells. Pour off and reserve the liquid from the pot.

Wash the broccoli and divide it into florets. Boil the broccoli in salted water until just tender and quickly transfer it to ice water to cool. Cut an X into the bottom of each tomato, boil them for about 10 seconds, then submerge them in ice water. Peel them, remove the seeds, and dice them. Skin, bone and dice the fish.

Sauté the fish in 3 tablespoon oil, seasoning it with salt and pepper. When the fish is cooked, add the marjoram with the mussels and their liquid. Then add the broccoli and tomatoes.

Boil the pasta in salted water until al dente. Reserve a bit of the pasta water and add it, along with the drained pasta, to the sauce. Let everything cook together for a minute, mixing well. Top it off with a drizzle of cold-pressed olive oil.

Difficulty

SALMON AND SPINACH LASAGNA

LASAGNE CON SALMONE E SPINACI

Preparation time: 1 hour + 20 minutes cooking time

Ingredients for 4 servings

FOR THE PASTA:

soft wheat flour (preferably Italian-type flour) 2 2/5 cups (300 g)

eggs 3

FOR THE PURÉE:

unsalted butter 3 tbsp (45 g)

flour 1/4 cup + 1 tbsp (40 g)

vegetable broth 2 cups (0.5 L)

salt to taste

FOR THE FILLING:

salmon fillet 1/2 lb (250 g)

fresh spinach 10 1/2 oz (300 g) about 10 cups

fresh ginger, grated 1 oz (30 g)

extra-virgin olive oil 1/3 cup + 2 tbsp (1 dl)

garlic 1 clove

salt and pepper to taste

Difficulty

Method

Pour the flour onto a cutting board or marble counter and create a well in the center. Break the eggs and drop them into the well. Start working them into the flour with a fork, then use your fingers and palms to knead the dough until it's smooth and consistent. Wrap it in plastic and refrigerate it for 30 minutes.

Roll the dough out to 1/32 inch (1 mm) thick and cut it into 4 x 4 3/4 inch (10 x 12 cm) rectangles. Boil the pasta in salted water and strain it when it's al dente. Cool it off immediately by putting it in a bowl of salted ice water. Then lay the rectangles out on cloths to dry. Preheat oven to 350° F (180° C).

Now make the sauce. Melt the unsalted butter in a deep pot, being careful not to let it burn. Add the flour, whisking continuously. Then start pouring in the broth, still whisking to avoid lumps. Bring it to a boil and maintain it for 1 minute to thicken the sauce slightly.

Sauté the whole garlic clove in half the oil. Add a teaspoon of grated ginger along with the spinach (pre-washed and drained). Season with salt and sauté it for a few seconds, but don't let it cook too much.

Remove the skin and any bones from the salmon. Dice it and sauté it in the remaining oil. Season it with salt and pepper to taste.

Spread some sauce in a greased baking dish and cover it with a layer of pasta. Cover it with a few spoonfuls of sauce, salmon pieces, and spinach. Continue in this order until all the ingredients have run out.

Bake the lasagna for about 20 minutes. Let it cool for 5-10 minutes and serve.

CELLENTANI PASTA SALAD WITH TUNA AND PEPPERS

INSALATA DI CELLENTANI CON TONNO E PEPERONI

Preparation time: 45 minutes + 8 minutes cooking time

Ingredients for 4 servings

cellentani pasta   12 oz (350 g)
fresh tuna   10 1/2 oz (300 g)
extra-virgin olive oil   2/3 cup (150 ml)
red bell peppers   1/2 lb (250 g) about
   2 medium
yellow bell peppers   1/2 lb (250 g)
   about 2 medium
capers   about 4 tbsp + 2 tsp (40 g)
minced parsley   1 tsp (0.5 g)
garlic   1 clove sliced thin
fresh thyme   2 sprigs
salt and pepper   to taste

Method

Remove the skin and any bones from the tuna. Let it marinate with one of the thyme sprigs and a bit of olive oil for 15 minutes. Grill it on a flat griddle, seasoning lightly with salt and pepper. Let it cool a bit and slice it against the grain into pieces about 1/8 inch (3-4 mm) thick.

Boil the pasta in salted water. When it's al dente, strain it and quickly run cold water over it to cool it off. Strain it again, very thoroughly. Transfer it to a large bowl and mix in a bit of olive oil so it doesn't stick together.

Wash the peppers and bake them in a preheated oven at 350° F (180° C) for about 20 minutes. Peel them, remove the seeds, and cut them into diamonds. Flavor them with the garlic (thinly sliced), thyme (stripped from the stem), and a drizzle of olive oil. Purée the capers with the oil.

In a large bowl combine the pasta with the peppers and a teaspoon of minced parsley. If necessary, add a bit of olive oil and a pinch of salt and pepper. Distribute it among the serving plates and top each one with a slice of tuna. Finish with a drizzle of caper oil.

Difficulty

CASTELLANE PASTA SALAD WITH SALMON AND FENNEL

INSALATA DI CASTELLANE CON SALMONE E FINOCCHIO

Preparation time: 25 minutes + 10 minutes cooking time

Ingredients for 4 servings

castellane pasta   12 oz (350 g)
salmon fillet   10 1/2 oz (300 g)
fennel bulb   8 1/2 oz (240 g) about
  1 medium
lemons   2
extra-virgin olive oil   1/3 cup (80 ml)
chives, minced   1 tbsp (0.1 g)
salt and black pepper   to taste

Method

Boil the pasta in salted water. When it's al dente, strain it and quickly run cold water over it to cool it off. Strain it again, very thoroughly. Transfer it to a large bowl and mix in a bit of olive oil so it doesn't stick together.

Zest the lemon, being careful not to include the white part. Slice the lemons in half and juice them. Slice the fennel very thinly and season it with a pinch of salt, ground pepper, and half the lemon juice. Remove the skin and any bones from the salmon fillet, then cut it into 3/4 inch (2 cm) cubes. Cook the fish over high heat on a flat griddle or nonstick pan with a bit of oil. Season it with salt and pepper and set it aside.

Mix the remaining lemon juice with the oil and a pinch of salt and pepper. Add the lemon zest and the minced chives. Combine all the ingredients with the pasta, mix well, and top it with the herbed lemon oil.

Difficulty

FUSILLI PASTA SALAD WITH VEGETABLES AND SQUID

INSALATA DI FUSILLI CON VERDURE E CALAMARI

Preparation time: 15 minutes + 10 minutes cooking time

Ingredients for 4 servings

fusilli   14 oz (400 g)

carrots, peeled and cut into thin strips
  5 1/3 oz (150 g) about
  2 medium

zucchini, cut into thin strips   14 oz (400
  g) about 2

artichokes   10 1/2 oz (300 g) about
  2 medium

**squid, cleaned and cut into very thin
  strips**   3

bunch of aromatic herbs

extra-virgin olive oil   1/4 cup (60 ml)

juice of lemon   1

salt and white pepper to taste

fresh Swiss chard   20 leaves (5 for
  serving)

Method

Wash the carrots and peel them. Clean the zucchini and dry them.

Remove the tough outer leaves from the artichokes. Cut them in half lengthwise and eliminate the "choke" from the center. Cut them into narrow strips and leave to soak in water with 1 tablespoon lemon juice to keep them from turning black. Then cut the carrots and zucchini into narrow strips.

Cook the pasta in a pan of salted boiling water. Five minutes before it is al dente, add the vegetables to the water with the pasta. Stir and cook for 3 minutes, then add the squid for the last 2 minutes. Drain, add a little oil, transfer everything to a tray and leave to cool. When it is cool, dress with the rest of the oil and lemon juice. Season with salt and white pepper. Serve on a bed of fresh Swiss chard.

Difficulty

DID YOU KNOW THAT ...

The first "artichoke queen," elected each year in Castroville, California, during the annual Artichoke Festival, was Marilyn Monroe in 1949.

CONCHIGLIE PASTA SALAD WITH PRAWNS

INSALATA DI CONCHIGLIE CON GAMBERI

Preparation time: 1 hour + 10 minutes cooking time

Ingredients for 4 servings

conchiglie pasta 12 oz (350 g)
cherry tomatoes 3 1/2 oz (100 g)
  about 6
king prawns 12
red onion 1 small
hot red pepper (fresh or dried) to taste
fresh basil 4-5 leaves cut into strips
garlic clove 1
extra-virgin olive oil 1/3 cup + 2 tbsp
  (100 ml)
salt and sugar to taste

Method

Boil the pasta in salted water. When it's very al dente, strain it and quickly run cold water over it to cool it off. Strain it again, very thoroughly. Transfer it to a large bowl and mix in a bit of olive oil so it doesn't stick together.

Wash the tomatoes, cut them in half, and arrange them in a pan. Sprinkle them with a handful of salt and a pinch of sugar. Drizzle them with olive oil and bake them at 200° F (100° C) until tender – about 45 minutes.

Shell and devein the prawns. Sauté the garlic with the oil and a few thin slices of fresh hot pepper. When the garlic is well browned, add the prawns and sauté them as well, but don't let them overcook.

Peel and dice the onion. Stew it in a separate pan on low heat with a bit of oil. If necessary, add a bit of water.

Add the tomatoes, prawns, and onion to the pasta. Mix well, adding some extra-virgin olive oil and fresh basil (cut into strips). Season with salt and pepper to taste and serve.

Difficulty

TOMATO SOUP
PAPPA AL POMODORO

Preparation time: 10 minutes + 30 minutes cooking time

Ingredients for 4 servings

mature vine tomatoes   1 lb (500 g)
yellow onion   7 oz (200 g) about 2
   small
water   1 cup (250 ml)
basil   about 1 cup (20 g), torn into pieces
garlic   3 cloves
chili powder   1/2 tsp
stale Tuscan type bread or other rustic
   bread   1 loaf (filone) weighing
   approximately 1 lb (400-500 g)
extra-virgin olive oil   6 tbsp + 2 tsp
   (100 ml)
salt and pepper   to taste

Method

Prepare the tomatoes by making an X-shaped incision on the bottom of each tomato and blanching them in boiling water for 10-15 seconds. Immediately dip the tomatoes in ice water, then peel them, cut them into four sections, remove the seeds and pass the pulp through a vegetable mill.

Chop the onion roughly and soften it in a saucepan in 4 tablespoon of the oil along with the whole peeled garlic cloves and the chili powder. Pour in the tomato purée and water, put on the saucepan lid and simmer over a low flame for 25-30 minutes. Season with salt and pepper.

Dice the stale bread and toast in a nonstick pan (without any fat) until the bread is completely dried out. Add to the soup with the basil, and continue cooking until the bread has softened and thickened the soup, about 10-15 minutes. Remove the garlic cloves.Drizzle the soup with a little extra-virgin olive oil and serve.

TYPES OF TOMATO

There are many types of tomato on the market, of different shapes, sizes and colors and with varying development of the plant and the fruit, each one being suitable for a particular culinary use. Salad tomatoes tend to be smooth and round or well segmented; sauce tomatoes are often long, fleshy, and deep red; tomatoes for juice or paste have a particularly strong scent; and tomatoes for drying or preserving in oil are generally small round or oval fruits.

Difficulty

ITALIAN VEGETABLE SOUP
MINESTRONE

Preparation time: 12 hours soaking time + 1 hour + 1 hour cooking time

Ingredients for 4 servings

leeks, sliced   3 1/5 oz (90 g)
celery, diced   2/3 cup (70 g)
potatoes, diced   7 oz (200 g) about 2 small
zucchini, diced   5 1/3 oz (150 g) about 1 medium
carrots, diced   2 4/5 oz (80 g) about 1 1/2 small
pumpkin, diced 3 1/2 oz (100 g)
borlotti beans   1/2 cup (100 g)
cannellini beans   1/2 cup (100 g)
savoy cabbage, sliced   3 1/2 oz (100 g)
green beans, sliced   3 1/2 oz (100 g)
fresh parsley   1 bunch
extra-virgin olive oil   1/3 cup (80 ml)
water   8 cups (2 l)
salt   to taste
Parmigiano-Reggiano cheese for garnish, if desired

Method

Soak the borlotti and cannellini beans separately in cold water overnight. The next day, change the water and cook the beans separately: starting with cold unsalted water, bring to a boil and cook until the beans are tender, about 30-45 minutes. Drain the beans and set aside. Bring 8 cups of water to a boil in a saucepan. In another saucepan, heat half the oil, add the vegetables and sauté util tender, about 4-5 minutes. Then pour in the boiling water, bring back to a boil, lower the flame and simmer for at least an hour. Add the drained beans toward the end of the cooking. Season with salt, if necessary, and sprinkle with parsley.

Drizzle each soup bowl with the rest of the olive oil, add grated Parmigiano cheese, to taste, and serve hot.

BEANS, FROM MEXICO TO EUROPE

This is a light, healthy dish with purifying properties. Vegetable minestrone is prepared all over Italy, with many variations from region to region. The variety of vegetables can change according to personal tastes, but beans are the ingredient that can never be lacking.

The bean (scientific name: Phaseolus vulgaris) is a member of the leguminous family. It originated in Central America, where it was cultivated 7,000 years ago. There are more than 500 varieties of beans, of which Borlotti and Cannellini are two of the best-known. These beans were brought to Europe by Christopher Columbus at the beginning of the 16th century and cultivated for their seeds, which were picked fresh (beans to shell) or dried, or for the whole legume to eat fresh (green beans). Gradually they replaced the Vigna beans of sub-Saharan origin that had dominated the tables of the ancient world.

Difficulty

VEGETABLE DUMPLINGS
GNUDI PROFUMATI AGLI ODORI DELL'ORTO

Preparation time: 30 minutes + 10 minutes cooking time

Ingredients for 4 servings

FOR THE GNUDI:

fresh spinach   14 oz (400 g)
fresh ricotta cheese   14 oz (400 g)
Parmigiano-Reggiano cheese   1 oz (30 g)
egg yolk   1
all-purpose flour   5 1/3 oz (150 g)
potato starch   1 1/3 oz (40 g)
nutmeg   to taste

FOR THE SAUCE:

tomato sauce   1/2 cup (1 dl)
butter   2 oz (60 g)
fresh sage   1/3 oz (10 g)

Method

Cook the spinach in a small amount of boiling salted water, drain it and leave to cool completely. Squeeze out any excess water and then chop finely.

On a work surface, add all the other ingredients to the spinach purée, and mix everything together thoroughly and rapidly. The resulting mixture must be uniform and soft. Leave the mixture to rest for about 30 minutes on a well-floured board. With the aid of a pastry bag with a smooth 3/4 inch- (2-cm) tip, form some lengths of pasta and cut them into 1 1/4-inch (3-cm) long pieces.

Cook the *gnudi* in abundant boiling salted water, and when they rise to the surface, strain them. In a large pan, melt the butter with the sage leaves. Lay the *gnudi* gently in the pan and toss them with the Parmigiano cheese.

Arrange the *gnudi* on the serving dish, and top with fresh tomato sauce and some basil leaves.

Difficulty

CHEF'S TIPS

The spinach must always be cooked in boiling salted water because in this way it maintains its green color.

EGG PASTA WITH PEAS
QUADRUCCI CON PISELLI

Preparation time: 30 minutes + 30 minutes cooking time

Ingredients for 4 servings

flour   1 3/4 cups (300 g)
eggs, lightly beaten   3
white wine   3 tbsp + 2 tsp (50 ml)
onion, finely chopped   1
fresh peas   1 3/4 lb (800 g)
bacon   7 oz (200 g)
salt   to taste

Method

Make a well with flour on a work surface. Add the eggs to the center of the well and gradually incorporate the flour. Knead the dough until it is smooth and elastic. Cover and leave the dough to rest for about 20 minutes. Roll the pasta out into thin sheets, cut it into strips 1/3 inch (1 cm) wide and then cut into squares. Leave the squares to dry on a well-floured tray.

Sauté the finely chopped onion in the oil over medium heat, add the bacon and gently fry for a few minutes; add the white wine and cook until it evaporates completely.

Add the peas and cover with water. Simmer for about 20 minutes and then add the *quadrucci*. Adjust the salt and continue cooking over medium heat until the pasta is al dente. The *quadrucci* should be served in a little of the broth or cooking liquid.

Difficulty

MAIN COURSES

CHAPTER THREE

ROASTED VEGETABLE MEDLEY WITH PECORINO TOSCANO

MOSAICO DI VERDURE CON PECORINO TOSCANO

Preparation time: 1 hour and 30 minutes + 20 minutes cooking time

Ingredients for 4 servings

eggplant   1/2 lb (250 g) about 1 small
zucchini   7 oz (200 g) about 1 medium
yellow bell pepper   7 oz (200 g) about
   1 large
red bell pepper   7 oz (200 g) about
   1 large
carrots   5 3/5 oz (160 g) about 2 small
red onions, preferably Tropea   5 1/3 oz
   (150 g) about 2 small
vine-ripened tomatoes   4 1/5 oz (120 g)
   about 1 1/2 small
**Pecorino Toscano cheese, plus more
   for serving**   3 1/2 oz (100 g)
extra-virgin olive oil, preferably Tuscan
   3 tbsp + 2 tsp (50 ml)
basil   to taste
salt   to taste

Method

Wash and slice the eggplant, carrots, onion and zucchini. Cut the tomatoes into wedges.

Grill the peppers whole, directly on a medium-high flame until charred all over and tender. Transfer to a bowl, cover with plastic wrap, and let rest for 15 minutes. Peel the skin from the peppers, remove the stem and seeds, then cut into wide strips. Put in a large bowl and set aside. Meanwhile, grill the sliced vegetables until browned and tender. Add them to the bowl with the peppers and toss with the olive oil, a pinch of salt and the hand-torn basil. Let marinate for at least 1 hour.

Arrange the vegetables in the center of a serving plate. Top with grated Pecorino flakes and drizzle with the olive oil.

THE COLORS OF FOOD

High gastronomy in the Middle Ages, Renaissance and Italian Baroque period assigned great importance to an element that, has only recently been taken into consideration again – the visual presentation of a dish. But in the Middle Ages, it wasn't just a matter of simple aesthetics. Colors actually had very specific symbolic meanings, and even in a culinary context they were a means to a particular end. Colors were incorporated through the use of ingredients with naturally bold colors and the addition of precious spices (like saffron) or artificial dyes. Regarding the symbolic meaning of various colors, white was associated with purity and balance. Red was a symbol of strength, instinct and carnality. Blue was associated with mysticism and ascension. And finally, yellow was the irrefutable king of aristocratic life in the past. As the color of gold and sunlight, it was considered a genuine terrestrial manifestation of the divine.

Difficulty

PIZZA MARGHERITA
PIZZA MARGHERITA

Preparation time: 30 minutes + 1 hour and 40 minutes rising time + 20 minutes cooking time

Ingredients for 8 servings

FOR THE DOUGH:

all-purpose flour   8 cups (1 kg)
fresh yeast   1 oz (30 g)
water, lukewarm   2 1/8 cups (500 ml)
sugar   1/3 oz (10 g)
salt   1/3 oz (10 g)

FOR THE TOPPING:

extra-virgin olive oil   2 tsp (10 ml)
buffalo-mozzarella cheese, diced
  1 3/4 lb (800 g)
fresh basil   40 leaves
fresh tomatoes, peeled   14 oz (400 g)
salt   to taste

Method

Dissolve the yeast and the sugar in the water, empty the flour onto a work surface and make a well in it, then pour the dissolved yeast into the center of the flour well. Start kneading, and after a while, add the salt. Knead until you have a smooth elastic dough. Set aside for a few minutes, then shape into 8 small balls, cover them so that the top part does not dry out, and leave them to rise.

When the dough has risen to twice its original size, roll out the balls of dough into round disks on a floured surface.

Make tomato purée by passing the peeled tomatoes through a food mill and pour out a ladleful of the tomato purée onto each disk of dough. Sprinkle diced mozzarella over the disks and drizzle with oil. Arrange basil leaves over the surface so that they are slightly covered with tomato purée to keep them from burning. Put the pizzas in the oven at 430° F (220° C).

Remove from the oven when the edges of the pizza are golden and crispy.

DID YOU KNOW THAT...

It is said that this pizza was created by Raffaele Esposito in 1889 in honor of Queen Margherita of Savoy, to bear witness to the affection of the people of Naples who saw her, as the young bride of Umberto I, ascend the throne in their own city.

CHEF'S TIPS

The Neapolitan pizza has three fundamental features: soft dough, a crisp edge and the topping.

Difficulty

SARDINIAN CABBAGE ROLLS

INVOLTINI SARDI

Preparation time: 20 minutes + 20 minutes cooking time

Ingredients for 4 servings

lean ground beef or pork   1 1/3 lb
  (600 g)
savoy cabbage with large leaves   1 head
extra-virgin olive oil   2 tbsp (30 ml)
white wine   1 cup (2 dl)
garlic   1 clove chopped
fresh sage   5 leaves chopped
parsley, chopped   3 tbsp
salt and pepper   to taste

Method

Mix together the ground meat with the garlic, sage, and parsley. Shape the mixture into small balls or cylinders about 1 1/4 inches (3 cm) long and 3/4 inch (2 cm) wide. Add salt and pepper to taste.

Break off the cabbage leaves and wash. Blanch the savoy cabbage leaves in boiling salted water until tender. Drain the leaves, immerse in ice water, then drain again. Wrap the leaves around the prepared meat.

Heat the oil in a large skillet over medium heat. Sauté the cabbage rolls until lightly browned, then add the white wine. Simmer until the wine evaporates. Cover the pan and cook, adding water if necessary, until the leaves are very tender.

Difficulty

CHICKEN CACCIATORE

POLLO ALLA CACCIATORA

Preparation time: 30 minutes + 30 minutes cooking time

Ingredients for 4 servings

chicken 1 whole, quartered 5 lb (2.26 kg)
flour 1 cup (136 g), for dredging
salt and black pepper to taste
extra-virgin olive oil 1/3 cup + 2 tbsp (100 ml)
yellow onion, diced 5 1/3 oz (150 g) about 1 large
carrots, chopped 2 4/5 oz (80 g) about 1 medium
celery stalk, chopped 1 3/4 oz (50 g), about 1 large
garlic 1 clove
tomatoes, seeded and chopped 2 1/4 lb (1 kg)
white wine 3/4 cup + 2 tbsp (200 ml)
chicken stock 1 cup (200 ml)
Bouquet garni 1 bay leaf, 1 sprig fresh rosemary, 1 sprig fresh sage, tied together with kitchen twine

Method

Rinse the chicken and pat dry. Lightly flour each piece, then season with salt and pepper. In a deep-sided frying pan over medium heat, heat 3 tablespoons of the oil (more if needed) until it is shimmering, then add the chicken pieces and fry until the skin is light golden brown, about 6 minutes per side. Remove the chicken pieces and set aside.

Heat the remaining oil in the pan and add the onions, carrot, celery, garlic, and bouquet garni. Cook until the onion and celery are translucent and the carrot is crisp-tender.

Return the chicken to the pan and stir in the wine. When the wine has evaporated, add the chopped tomatoes and the stock.

Let simmer on low heat for at least 30 minutes, until the chicken is cooked through and tender and the sauce is thick and fragrant. (During cooking, add more stock as needed to keep the consistency of the sauce.) Before serving, remove the bouquet garni and garlic clove.

Serve the chicken with plenty of sauce.

Difficulty

CHICKEN AND POTATO SALAD
INSALATA DI POLLO E PATATE

Preparation time: 15 minutes + 20 minutes cooking time + 30 minutes cooling time

Ingredients for 4 servings

red or white potatoes   1/3 lb (150 g)
boneless chicken breasts   1 lb (400 g)
mixed salad greens   7 oz (200 g) about
   1 package
balsamic vinegar   2/3 cup (150 ml)
extra-virgin olive oil   3 1/2 tbsp (50 ml)
fresh sage   2-3 leaves, chopped
sprig of rosemary, chopped
salt and black pepper   to taste

Method

Wash the chicken breasts and pat dry. In a skillet over medium heat, place the chicken breasts, 2 tablespoons of the balsamic vinegar, half of the herbs, a pinch of salt and just enough water to cover. Bring to a boil and simmer until the chicken is cooked through, about 20 minutes. Remove the chicken from the liquid and let it cool.

Peel the potatoes and boil in salted water until cooked but still firm, about 15 minutes. Let cool and cut into wedges.

Cut the chicken into strips and toss with 2 tablespoons of the oil, the chopped herbs and a sprinkling of freshly ground pepper.

Whisk together the remaining oil and balsamic vinegar with a pinch of salt. Toss with the salad greens in a large bowl and add the chicken and potato wedges. Toss lightly and serve.

Difficulty

CHICKEN MARSALA WITH PEPPERS

POLLO AL MARSALA E PEPERONI

Preparation time: 30 minutes + 30 minutes cooking time

Ingredients for 4 servings

chicken   1 whole, cut into 8 pieces 5 lb
(2.26 kg)
extra-virgin olive oil   1/3 cup + 2 tbsp
(100 ml)
red bell pepper sliced into strips   1/2
lb (250 g) about 1 1/2 large
yellow bell pepper sliced into strips
1/2 lb (250 g) about 1 1/2 large
yellow onion sliced   3 1/2 oz (100 g),
1 medium
Marsala wine   3/4 cup + 2 tbsp (200
ml)
chicken stock   1 1/4 cups (300 ml)
flour   as needed
cornstarch   as needed
sprig of rosemary
salt and black pepper   to taste

Method

Rinse the chicken pieces and pat them dry. Lightly flour the chicken, then season with salt and pepper. In a deep-sided frying pan over medium heat, heat 4 tablespoons of the oil (more if needed) until it is shimmering, then add the chicken pieces and fry until the skin is light golden brown, about 6 minutes per side. Remove the chicken pieces and set aside.

Add the remaining oil to a large frying pan along with the rosemary and onion. Cook over medium heat until the onion is translucent and slightly caramelized. Add the chicken pieces, then pour in the Marsala and cook over medium-high until the wine evaporates. Reduce the heat and add the peppers and chicken stock to the pan. Simmer for about 30 minutes, until the sauce is fragrant and the flavors have melded.

If you prefer a thicker sauce, dissolve a pinch of cornstarch in a few drops of water and stir it in at the very end.

CHICKEN

The modern domestic chicken originated in Asia and spread throughout Europe by way of Greece. It was very popular in ancient Rome and the Romans realized the importance of an animal's diet in producing the best meat. They apparently fed poultry with a mixture of barley flour and water, or even wheat bread soaked in good wine. Of course, these were strategies for the kitchens of aristocrats, not plebeians. Chicken went through a dark period in the High Middle Ages, when the new Celtic and Germanic rulers imposed alternative alimentary ideals. It came back in style around 1400, when the increasing sophistication of European courts coincided with the revival and celebration of white meat.

Difficulty

STUFFED BREAST OF VEAL

CIMA ALLA GENOVESE

Preparation time: 1 hour + 2 hours cooking time

Ingredients for 4 servings

eggs 3
peas 1 3/4 oz (50 g)
dried porcini mushrooms 1 3/4 oz
  (50 g)
lean veal, minced 3 1/2 oz (100 g)
marjoram 1 tsp (0.6 grams) + more to
  taste
parmesan cheese, grated 1 3/4 oz
  (50 g)
grated nutmeg 1/8 tsp (0.3 grams) +
  more to taste
garlic 1 clove chopped fine
pine nuts 3 1/2 oz (100 g)
salt and black pepper to taste
breast of veal 1 lb 10 oz (750 g)

Method

Boil the eggs for about 6 minutes. Cool them and remove the shells. Soak the mushrooms in lukewarm water; drain and then wring them out and chop them. Place the peas in a small saucepan and add salted water to cover. Boil the peas until they are bright green and crisp tender, about 2 minutes. Drain and set aside.

In a large bowl, combine the minced veal, marjoram, cheese, nutmeg, garlic, mushrooms, pine nuts and peas. Season with salt and pepper and mix well.

Cut a slit into the veal breast to create a pocket, and stuff with the veal mixture and the whole boiled eggs. Sew the pocket closed with twine and a kitchen needle; wrap the whole breast in a layer of cheesecloth, then tie the bundle with kitchen twine. Place the meat in a large saucepan with enough cold water to cover. Bring to a boil and simmer for 2 hours. Let the veal cool in the cooking water, then remove the twine and cloth. Cut into thick slices, and serve.

"SUNG CIMA"

After trofie al pesto, cima is probably the most famous Ligurian dish, specifically from Genoa. It is a very old main course and it goes back to a time when, in an effort not to waste any meat, the people of Liguria would prepare a tasty and nutritious roast by stuffing it with whatever they had at home. The famous Genoese singer and songwriter Fabrizio De André was particularly fond of this dish; he and his colleague Ivano Fossati dedicated a song to it in the Genoese dialect, called "A çimma." The lyrics of the song do not explore the ingredients of the dish but highlight the importance of it being baptized with herbs, first and foremost with marjoram, and how preparing it has always been a delicate and complex ritual for the housewives of Liguria.

Difficulty

FISH SKEWERS IN SALMORIGLIO SAUCE

SPIEDINI DI PESCE AL SALMORIGLIO

Preparation time: 45 minutes + 10 minutes cooking time

Ingredients for 4 servings

scallops 8
shrimp, shelled and deveined 8 medium
anglerfish or monkfish fillet 1/2 lb
   (200 g)
mullet or any firm-fleshed white fish, 2
   fillets 1/2 lb (200 g) each
juice of 2 lemons
garlic 1 clove minced
parsley, chopped 1 tbsp (0.5 g)
fresh oregano, chopped 1 tsp (1.25 g)
extra-virgin olive oil 3/4 cup + 2 tbsp
   (200 ml)
water 3 1/2 tbsp (50 ml)
salt and black pepper to taste

Method

Cube the anglerfish and slide it onto skewers, alternating with the scallops, shrimp and mullet fillets.

For the sauce: Pour the oil into a bowl and whisk in the lemon juice and hot water, mixing vigorously. Add the garlic and parsley. Heat the mixture in a double boiler for 5-6 minutes, whisking continuously.

Drizzle some salmoriglio over the skewers, then grill over medium-high heat, basting with more salmoriglio as they cook. Season them with salt, pepper and fresh oregano.

Serve 2 skewers per person, topping them with the remaining salmoriglio.

Difficulty

STUFFED SARDINES
SARDE A BECCAFICO

Preparation time: 40 minutes + 20 minutes cooking time

Ingredients for 4 servings

whole sardines   17 1/2 oz (500 g)
   about 12 large
bread crumbs   1/2 cup (100 g)
salt-packed anchovies, deboned,
   desalted and chopped 2
pine nuts   2/3 oz (20 g)
raisins   2/3 oz (20 g)
parsley, chopped   1 tbsp
extra-virgin olive oil   4 tbsp (50 ml) +
   more for drizzling
bay leaves   to taste (twelve)
salt and black pepper   to taste

Method

Heat 3 tablespoons of the oil in a skillet and add the bread crumbs. Sauté until they start to brown, then let them cool. Add the parsley, pine nuts, raisins and anchovies, season with salt and pepper, and mix well. Clean the sardines then cut them lengthwise and open them up like a book, skin-side down. Put a little of the mixture on each sardine so that the skin remains on the outside, and then roll them up starting from the head so that the tail is left outside. Secure the rolls with a toothpick.

Heat the oven to 350 °F (180 °C). Oil a baking pan. Arrange the twelve bay leaves evenly on the pan, and place a sardine roll atop each one. Drizzle with the rest of the oil and bake for about 20 minutes, until the tops of the sardines are golden.

STUFFED SARDINES

This is a tasty main dish of Sicilian origin; sarde a beccafico *take their name from "beccafichi," small birds that are very greedy for figs. They are and commonly found in the fields of Sicily, where they eat this sweet fruit in the summer and grow quite plump.*
Some say this dish is so called because the stuffed sardines resemble beccafichi. Others claim it is the poor man's version of a delicacy of noble origin: the prized beccafichi stuffed with sardines. The poor man's version merely used the main ingredient for the stuffing, which was decidedly more economical than the beccafichi themselves, and stuffed it with bread crumbs and orange or lemon juice. Subsequently the stuffing was enriched with anchovy fillets, pine nuts and raisins, and flavored with parsley and bay leaves. Among the many variations of sarde a beccafico *that are found in Sicily, Catania's version replaces the bread crumbs with grated Pecorino and the flavors the stuffing with garlic and chopped onion.*

Difficulty

ROASTED SCALLOPS WITH PURÉED PEAS

CAPESANTE ARROSTITE CON PUREA DI PISELLI

Preparation time: 35 minutes + 5 minutes cooking time

Ingredients for 4 servings

scallops   12
peas   14 oz (400 g) about 2 3/4 cups
cuttlefish ink (optional)   1/5 oz (5 g)
extra-virgin olive oil   1/3 cup + 1 tbsp
  (90 ml)
salt and pepper   to taste

Method

Boil the peas in salted water. Strain them and blend them in a food processor, adding a ladleful of the water they were cooked in. Then pass them through a fine mesh strainer, which should result in a fairly dense purée. Season it with 1/3 of the oil and salt and pepper to taste.

Dilute the cuttlefish ink with 1/3 of the olive oil.

Open the shells, remove the scallops and rinse them well. Sear them in a very hot pan with the remaining oil, seasoning with salt and pepper to taste.

When they're done (they should cook in about 5 minutes), serve the scallops over a layer of puréed peas. Top them with the mixture of olive oil and cuttlefish ink.

SCALLOPS

The history of scallops is very tightly woven with that of Christianity and religious liturgy. In fact, they're also known as "shells of St. James." Pilgrims who traveled to Santiago de Compostela (in Galicia) would collect scallop shells along the beaches and present them upon returning, both as proof of their journey and a way to avoid tolls and tallages.
Even art history provides a splendid image of this jewel of nature – Botticelli's Venus rising from a scallop shell. Scallops are the third most consumed mollusk in the world. They are extremely versatile, lending themselves to an infinite variety of recipes. And given their beauty, they are also a wonderful decorative element that greatly contributes to the table's aesthetic appeal.

Difficulty

STUFFED SQUID
CALAMARI FARCITI

Preparation time: 30 minutes + 15 minutes cooking time

Ingredients for 4 servings

medium squid   4
shrimp, peeled and deveined   4
bread crumbs   1/3 cup (40 g)
lemon (zest and juice)   1
egg white   1
garlic clove   half
minced parsley   1 tbsp (0.5 g)
mixed greens   3 1/2 oz (100 g)
extra-virgin olive oil   3 tbsp (40 ml)
salt and pepper   to taste

Method

Clean and rinse the squid and shrimp. Cut the tentacles off the squid and boil them in water with the lemon juice. Roughly chop the tentacles and finely chop the shrimp.

Mince the garlic and parsley and combine them with the bread crumbs. Mix in the egg white, tentacles, shrimp, a pinch of lemon zest and salt and pepper to taste. Stuff the squid bodies with this filling, using toothpicks to hold them closed.

Lightly grease a pan with olive oil and arrange the squid inside. Bake them in a 350° F (170-180° C) oven until cooked through, about 15 minutes. Slice the squid and garnish each serving with mixed greens. Top it off with a drizzle of the olive oil.

SALAD GREENS

Unlike other European culinary traditions, Italian cuisine is largely characterized by the use of vegetables, root vegetables, herbs (wild and cultivated) and agricultural products in general. This Italian custom has its roots in specific social, economic and climactic conditions, but it quickly became a genuine preference. There is a "salad law" that should be followed when dressing salads, in order to fully honor the palate. First, the greens must be carefully washed and dried, then arranged on a plate that has already been sprinkled with a bit of salt. Then salt should be sprinkled over the greens and a good amount of olive oil should be drizzled on top. It needs to be carefully tossed so that each leaf "gets some oil" and finished with a generous dash of vinegar. If you don't follow this procedure, the delicious salad greens remain only "good for duck food."

Difficulty

ANGLERFISH SALAD WITH PANTELLERIAN CAPERS
INSALATA DI RANA PESCATRICE CON CAPPERI DI PANTELLERIA

Preparation time: 30 minutes + 5 minutes cooking time

Ingredients for 4 servings

mixed greens, torn   7 oz (200 g)

carrot, sliced   1 3/4 oz (50 g) about
  1 small

fennel bulb, thinly sliced   2 4/5 oz
  (80 g) about 1/3 medium

**anglerfish or halibut, cut into 1/4-inch
  thick slices**   2 lbs (1 kg)

pickled capers, rinsed and drained
  2 tbsp (20 g)

minced parsley   2 tbsp (1 g)

extra-virgin olive oil   1/3 cup + 2 tbsp
  (100 ml)

balsamic vinegar (aged 12 years)   1/2
  tsp (3 ml)

salt and white pepper   to taste

mint   4-5 leaves

chives   12 leaves

basil   4-5 leaves

marjoram   1 sprig

Difficulty

Method

Clean all the vegetables and greens. Rinse the capers well and strain them. In a bowl, toss together the mixed greens, carrot, and fennel.

Clean the anglerfish, removing the skin and bones. Slice the fish in 1/4-inch (0.5 cm) thick pieces. Heat 1 tablespoon + 2 teaspoon of the oil over medium heat, add the slices of fish and cook until golden brown on both sides and cooked through. Season generously with salt and pepper.

Tear the greens in pieces and arrange them in the center of a plate. Place the fish on top with the capers and minced parsley. Season with balsamic vinegar, remaining extra-virgin olive oil, salt and pepper.

BALMS AND ELIXIRS

The traditional balsamic vinegar of Modena has been a DOP (Protected Designation of Origin) product for three decades; its cultural, historical, and gastronomic value has been recognized and considered almost equivalent to archeological or artistic heritage. It is also a very ancient product, documented since at least the 11th century.

In the past, the term acetum referred to an array of acetic condiments derived from the fermentation of must or wine, which were very popular in an era when recipes called for a predominance of sweet or sour flavors. The vinegar is aged for years in wooden barrels (juniper, chestnut, oak, mulberry), which imbue the liquid they contain with scents and fragrances – no other aromas are added.

The word "balsamic" comes from balsamico (balm) and for centuries it was actually used for therapeutic purposes. It was considered a genuine elixir, and perhaps that's part of the reason the producers have always been extremely careful about guarding the secrets of production passed down to them.

SWORDFISH IN SALMORIGLIO SAUCE

PESCE SPADA AL SALMORIGLIO

Preparation time: 15 minutes + 5 minutes cooking time

Ingredients for 4 servings

swordfish fillet 1 1/3 lbs (600 g)
lemon 2
garlic 1 clove, chopped
parsley 1 tbsp (0.5 g), chopped
oregano 1 tsp (1.25 g), chopped
extra-virgin olive oil scant 1 cup
  (250 ml)
water 3 tbsp + 2 tsp (50 ml)
salt and pepper to taste

Method

Cut the swordfish fillet into four slices.

For the salmoriglio sauce: Put the oil, lemon juice and hot water in a bowl and whisk together. Add the chopped garlic, parsley and oregano, whisking the mixture continuosly for 5-6 minutes in a bain-marie (a bowl set into a bowl or saucepan of very warm water.) Brush the slices of fish with the salmoriglio sauce and cook on a griddle or grill for a few minutes, brushing the fish with the sauce until it is golden brown on both sides and cooked through. Season with salt and pepper.

Brush with the sauce once again and serve.

EATEN SINCE PREHISTORIC TIMES

Swordfish is a typical Sicilian dish and salmoriglio sauce with which it is served is as well. This traditional sauce, whose name is the Italian adaptation of the Sicilian term sammurigghiu, is usually used to accompany grilled meat or fish. The traditional recipe involves emulsifying the hot water, oil and lemon juice in a bowl but on the Aeolian Islands, a sauce made with citrus fruits, red wine, parsley and rosemary is used for roast meats.
Swordfish is caught in the area around the Straits of Messina and is a prized symbol of Sicilian and Calabrian cuisine. In these regions, this prized fish is eaten roasted, smoked in carpaccio or marinated. It seems that fishing for swordfish in this small stretch of sea was done even in prehistoric times. Indeed, ruins of villages have come to light, dating back to the Bronze Age, with swordfish bones among the remains of food.

Difficulty

SIMPLE POACHED SEA BASS
BRANZINO ALL'ACQUA PAZZA

Preparation time: 15 minutes + 20 minutes cooking time

Ingredients for 4 servings

sea bass fillets 3.3 lbs (1.5 kg)
yellow onions, thinly sliced 5 1/3 oz
  (150 g), about 2 small
cherry tomatoes 1/2 lb (250 g) about
  15
extra-virgin olive oil 3 1/2 tbsp (50 ml)
basil 5 leaves
garlic 2 cloves
water 3/4 cup + 2 tbsp (200 ml)
salt and black pepper to taste

Method

For the acqua pazza: Sauté the onion, garlic and basil in the oil until the onion is translucent. Add the tomatoes and water and let everything cook for about 10 minutes.

Season the fish with salt and pepper, then place it in the acqua pazza and cook over medium heat, turning once, about 6-8 minutes per side, until the fish is cooked through.

Ladle fish and broth into bowls and serve.

ACQUA PAZZA

Acqua pazza (literally, "crazy water") was originally a traditional maritime soup. Fishermen would take the small discarded fish that remained tangled in the nets (and therefore went unsold) and boil them in seawater with vegetables and spices. The recipe got its name, which is still used today, when a bit of white wine was added to the water. Popular throughout the Mediterranean, especially in Provence and southern Italy, it was a frugal yet wholesome one-course meal usually eaten with hard tack biscuits called gallette. *It's important to note that every region of Italy offers fish dishes modeled on this basic soup — water, salt, and spices, occasionally enriched with eggs, cheese, scraps of meat, or bones, depending on the products readily available in the area.*

Difficulty

GROUPER MATALOTTA-STYLE

CERNIA ALLA MATALOTTA

Preparation time: 25 minutes + 15 minutes cooking time

Ingredients for 4 servings

grouper filets   1 3/4 lb (800 g)
all-purpose flour   1/2 cup (60 g)
tomatoes, quartered   7 oz (200 g)
onion, thinly sliced   3 1/2 oz (100 g)
garlic, thinly sliced   1/5 oz (5 g)
bay leaf   1
almonds   1 oz (30 g)
parsley, chopped   1/3 oz (8 g)
white wine   1/2 cup (1 dl)
extra-virgin olive oil   3 tbsp + 2 tsp
  (50 ml)
salt and pepper   to taste
fish broth   1/2 cup (1 dl)
**button mushrooms, cleaned and thinly
  sliced**   3 1/2 oz (100 g)

FOR THE GARNISH:
zucchini, sliced   3 1/2 oz (100 g)
sliced almonds   to taste
**mixed peppers, sliced into 1/2-inch
  pieces**   2 1/2 oz (80 g)

Method

In a tray with low edges flour the grouper filets.

Sauté half the thinly sliced onion and garlic in oil for 1 minute. Add filets and fry gently. Add the white wine and simmer until it evaporates. Add the quartered tomatoes, season with salt and pepper and add fish broth, bay leaf and thinly sliced mushrooms. Add the chopped parsley and cook over low heat for 5 minutes. Salt the remaining onion with the sliced zucchini separately. Add the chopped peppers, add salt and sauté over a high flame. Finally, add the almonds.

Arrange on a serving dish by placing the filets first, then garnishing with the vegetables.

Difficulty

LIGURIAN SEAFOOD WITH VEGETABLES
CAPPON MAGRO

Preparation time: 2 hours

Ingredients for 4 servings

bread 4 slices, toasted
black cod 1 3/4 lbs (800 g)
spiny lobster 1 2/3 lbs (750 g)
prawns 4
anchovies 2, rinsed and deboned
hard boiled eggs 2
cauliflower 10 1/2 oz (300 g)
green beans 3 1/2 oz or 18 beans (100 g)
potatoes 1 small 3 1/2 oz (100 g)
carrots 2 small 3 1/2 oz (100 g)
celery 1 3/4 oz (50 g) about 2 stalks
beets 7 oz (200 g)
white turnips 7 oz (200 g) about 1 small
mushrooms in oil 2 oz (60 g)
artichokes 10 1/2 oz (300 g) about
  2 medium
green olives 12
lemon 1
extra-virgin olive oil 2 tbsp + 2 tsp (40 ml)
white wine vinegar 3 tbsp + 2 tsp (50 ml)
salt to taste
FOR THE SAUCE:
parsley 2 tsp (8 g)
bread without crust 2/3 oz (20 g)
vinegar 1 tbsp (15 ml)
pine nuts 2 tbsp (15 g)
salt-packed anchovies 1/2 oz (15 g)
capers 2 tbsp (15 g)
extra-virgin olive oil 1 tbsp (15 ml)
green olives, pitted 1/3 oz (10 g) about
  5 olives
garlic 1 clove
**hard boiled
  egg yolks** 2
salt to taste

Difficulty

Method

To prepare the sauce, soften the bread by soaking it in vinegar. Then wring it out and blend it in a food processor together with the deboned and rinsed anchovies, the clove of garlic, two hard-boiled egg yolks, capers, olives, pine nuts, parsley and a little extra-virgin olive oil. Add salt to taste.

Wash and trim the cauliflower, green beans, celery and carrots and boil them in salted water until crisp-tender. Wash, peel, and cut the potatoes, turnips, beetroot and artichokes in half and boil them separately. Dice or slice the vegetables and add half of the oil, salt and a drop of vinegar.

Poach the fish in salted water. Boil the spiny lobster and the prawns separately. Cut the fish into pieces. Shell and slice the flesh of the spiny lobster and prawns. Make a dressing with the remaining oil, the juice of one lemon and a pinch of salt.

Arrange the ingredients in a serving dish in alternate layers of vegetables and fish, and dress each layer with a little of the sauce.

Finish with the spiny lobster medallions, the prawns, an anchovy per portion, the sliced mosciame or bottarga, the sliced hard boiled eggs, the olives and the mushrooms in oil. Pour the remaining sauce over the dish. Cappon magro should be served with sea biscuits or slices of toast that have been sprinkled with a few drops of vinegar.

SALAD & VEGETABLES

CHAPTER FOUR

ARTICHOKE SALAD WITH PARMIGIANO-REGGIANO CHEESE

INSALATA DI CARCIOFI CON PARMIGIANO-REGGIANO

Preparation time: 20 minutes

Ingredients for 4 servings

artichokes   20 4/5 oz (600 g) about
 4 medium
Parmigiano-Reggiano cheese, shaved
 1 cup + 3 tbsp (120 g)
juice of 2 lemons
mint leaves, torn into pieces   4-5
extra-virgin olive oil, preferably
 Ligurian   3 tbsp + 2 tsp (50 ml)
salt and pepper   to taste

Method

Clean the artichokes, removing the outer leaves and spines. Peel the stems and soak the artichokes in a mixture of water and lemon juice for 15 minutes. Grate or slice the Parmigiano into thin shavings.

Combine 1-2 tablespoons lemon juice, the olive oil and a pinch of salt and pepper.

Cut the artichokes in half, and if necessary remove the tough inner fibers. Slice them very thinly and dress them with the lemon and olive oil emulsion.

Arrange the artichokes in the center of the plate. Top them with Parmigiano, hand-torn mint leaves and a drizzle of cold-pressed olive oil.

ARTICHOKES

As Montaigne noted with great surprise in The Journal of Montaigne's Travels in Italy *from the late 16th century, the artichoke (*Cynara scolymus*) is often eaten raw in Italy. Likely derived from the wild cardoon, Italians' extraordinary agricultural skills and incomparably inventive gastronomy led to the exceptional product that we know today. Once again, humans stubbornly wanted to modify nature, through a series of botanical grafting experiments, to fit their own tastes. The use of artichokes began to spread in the 16th century, and like all little known plants it was immediately assigned symbolic meanings and curious medical and scientific beliefs. For example, the artichoke's reputation as a potent aphrodisiac may be why it was forbidden to young people from good families.*

Difficulty

ANCHOVY SALAD WITH FRESH VEGETABLES

CONDIGLIONE

Preparation time: 20 minutes

Ingredients for 4 servings

tomatoes, not too ripe   20 4/5 oz (600 g) about 3 1/2 large
yellow bell peppers   7 oz (200 g) about 1 1/2 large
cucumber   7 oz (200 g) about 1 small
red onions   5 1/3 oz (150 g) about 2 small
anchovies packed in salt, rinsed, bones removed and cut in half   1 1/3 oz (40 g)
black olives, preferably Ligurian   1 3/4 oz (50 g) about 12 large
basil leaves, torn into pieces   4-5
red wine vinegar   1 tbsp (15 ml)
extra-virgin olive oil, preferably Ligurian   3 1/2 tbsp (50 ml)
garlic   1 clove
salt   to taste

Difficulty

Method

Rinse the anchovies and remove the bones. Clean and rinse all the vegetables. Finely slice the onion, cut the peppers into small strips, cut the cucumber into rounds and cut the tomatoes into slices or wedges.

Place all the vegetables in a large salad bowl and add the olives, anchovies, basil and whole garlic clove (or thinly sliced if you prefer a more intense flavor).

Season the salad with salt, oil and vinegar. Let everything marinate for about 10 minutes, then serve.

ITALIAN DRESSING

The typical Italian predilection for mixed greens, salads and vegetables (raw or cooked) is unquestionable. But reading various works from the past brings another aspect to light, one that is not given enough attention. Vegetable preparation methods, various modes of consumption (even types of chewing) and traditional seasonings and dressings are all based on cultural factors. Bartolomeo Sacchi, also called Platina, was a 15th century humanist and gastronomer. In his treatise De Honesta Voluptate, he describes the Italian dressing par excellence at length and in great detail: First a generous dose of salt, then high quality oil (distributed generously by hand), followed by a dash of good vinegar. After mixing thoroughly, the vegetables should be left to marinate, allowing the flavors and aromas to mingle to perfection. It's no coincidence that grapes and olives, elements of the famous Mediterranean triad, are combined in even the simplest of condiments.

CHRISTMAS SALAD
INSALATA DI NATALE

Preparation time: 25 minutes

Ingredients for 4 servings

sweet chicory, roughly chopped
  10 1/2 oz (300 g)
celery, sliced 10 1/2 oz (300 g)
capers in brine, rinsed 2 tbsp (17 g)
green olives, chopped 2 tbsp (20 g)
orange, peeled and cut into segments 1
lemon, peeled and cut into segments 1
the seeds from 1 pomegranate
extra-virgin olive oil 2 tbsp (30 ml)
salt to taste

Difficulty

Method

Boil the chicory and celery separately until very tender. Drain and set aside to cool. Mix together the chicory, celery, capers, olives, and olive oil. Combine well and arrange on a serving dish. Top with the orange and lemon segments and then garnish with pomegranate seeds.

LEMONS IN COOKING

How would we manage in the kitchen without lemons? Lemons are precious not just because of their unmistakable aroma but also because of their properties, which aid the digestion of certain foods, like meat, fish dishes and fried food. After a meal, lemon is ideal in a hot tisane or in a liqueur like traditional Limoncello. By adding a few drops of lemon juice to coffee and barley coffee, you obtain an invigorating drink.

Lemon adds a touch of class to pasta and rice dishes, both hot and cold, it takes away from game that "gamey" taste that is not appreciated by everybody, and it is an excellent substitute for vinegar in a dressing. It is perfect as a salad dressing and for making mayonnaise with a more delicate flavor. A few drops of lemon juice also help to remove excess grease from dressings and greasy foods in general, making them lighter and easier to digest. This citrus fruit is indispensable for its capacity to prevent the oxidation of freshly cut fruit and vegetables, i.e., their tendency to turn brown. For this reason, a little lemon juice is added to the water when you clean artichokes or carrots; likewise, lemon juice is added to fruit salads.

Lemon juice can also lightly "cook" foods: it is used for raw preparations of fish and meat, such as tartare or carpaccio. Just as the flesh of lemons is used as a dressing for Mediterranean salads and cooked vegetables, the zest, grated or diced, adds additional flavor to confectioner's cream and cakes.

ORANGE SALAD
INSALATA DI ARANCE

Preparation time: 30 minutes

Ingredients for 4 servings

tarocco blood oranges   1 lb (450 g)
   about 2 medium
lemon   1
endive   1 head, thinly sliced
extra-virgin olive oil   3 tbsp + 2 tsp
   (50 ml)
salt and pepper   to taste

Method

With a small, sharp knife, cut the peel and white membrane from oranges and lemon. Slice the fruit crosswise 1/8 to 1/4 inch thick and discard seeds, or divide the fruit into segments (reserve any the juice that escapes.)

In a small bowl, whisk together the reserved juice with salt, pepper and extra-virgin olive oil.

Dress the fruit with the freshly made dressing and serve on a bed of endive leaves or in bowls made from hollowed-out orange halves.

ELEPHANTS' FAVORITE FRUIT

This delicate tasty orange salad is typical of Sicilian cuisine and is ideal for festive Christmas meals and during the winter months when Tarocco oranges can be found (this is a prized variety, characterized by a red streaked flesh and usually no seeds). It is perfect as a side dish, especially to accompany particularly fatty meats.

Native to China and Southeast Asia, the sweet orange is the fruit of the orange tree (Citrus aurantium), an evergreen that can reach 39 feet (12 meters) in height. The orange, whose name derives from the Persian narang, which in turn derives from the Sanskrit term nagaranja, meaning "the elephants' favorite fruit," arrived in Europe in the 14th century, imported by Portuguese explorers, even though some ancient documents refer to it as early as the 1st century A.D.: it was called melarancia (apple orange) and cultivated in Sicily. Perhaps the orange arrived in the Mediterranean in ancient times via the Silk Road and found a favorable climate for its cultivation on the warm Italian island. For some reason, however, its production stopped after some time. It was the Portuguese who brought it back to Europe in the Middle Ages. Even today, in the dialects of many Italian regions, the orange is still called portogallo (Portugal).

Difficulty

SALAD WITH PINK GRAPEFRUIT, YOUNG SPINACH AND WALNUTS

INSALATA DI POMPELMO ROSA, SPINACI NOVELLI E NOCI

Preparation time: 15 minutes

Ingredients for 4 servings

pink grapefruit   2
walnuts, shelled and roughly
  chopped   16
young spinach leaves fresh   7 oz (200 g)
extra-virgin olive oil   3 1/2 tbsp (50 ml)
salt and black pepper   to taste

Method

Peel the grapefruit and divide into segments. Squeeze the remaining pulp into a container; add the salt and extra-virgin olive oil to the grapefruit juice to make a citronette dressing. Wash and dry the spinach carefully. Add the citronette dressing to the spinach in a bowl.

Arrange the salad on a plate and garnish with the walnuts and grapefruit segments.

Before serving, sprinkle with ground black pepper.

Difficulty

DID YOU KNOW THAT...

Among the ingredients of this unusual spring salad are walnuts. Since ancient times they have been a symbol of life.
In Roman times they used to be thrown at the bride and groom because their sound covered the shouts of the bride during her simulated kidnapping. She then had to throw the walnuts because their falling and bouncing was a sign of good fortune.
Such traditions have not been completely lost in Europe although rice is now thrown at weddings in Italy.

MARINATED FRIED ZUCCHINI

ZUCCHINE A SCAPECE

Preparation time: 30 minutes + 12 hours to marinate

Ingredients for 4 servings

zucchini, cut into small strips 1 lb
(500 g) about 2 1/2 medium
white wine vinegar 1/3 cup + 2 tbsp
(100 ml)
water 1/3 cup + 2 tbsp (100 ml)
mint, roughly chopped 1 bunch
garlic 1 clove thinly sliced
peppercorns 10
extra-virgin olive oil for frying
salt to taste

Method

Wash the zucchini and cut them into small strips. Heat 1/2 inch of oil in a skillet and fry the zucchini (a few at a time) until they're golden brown. Remove them with a perforated spoon to a plate lined with paper towels to drain. Season them with salt and arrange them in a bowl, adding the roughly chopped mint.

Boil the water with the vinegar, pepper and thinly sliced garlic for 5 to 6 minutes. You can alter the water-to-vinegar ratio depending on how much acidity you prefer. Pour the hot marinade over the zucchini. Once cooled, store in the refrigerator. Serve the next day, cold or at room temperature.

THE STRANGE CASE OF SCAPECE

Scapece (food that's been fried and marinated) is a cooking method geared toward the preservation and eventual transport of certain products. Apicio was a Roman cook from the Imperial Age, and in De re coquinaria (I, 9) he had already suggested frying fish in oil, draining them and immediately pouring a large amount of vinegar over them. This procedure is still associated with the name of the inventor, and the term scapece may come from a contraction of the Latin phrase esca Apicii, meaning "food of Apicio." But it's more likely a word of Arabic origin which came to Italy via the Spanish escabeche. In the 13th century, scapece appeared on the royal table. It seems that Federico II of Svevia was very fond of fish cooked this way and the royal chef, Bernardo, was an expert at it. Cookbooks from the 14th century place scapece back among the masses, specifically in taverns, where it was called schibezia a tav-ernaio (a bit like saying "tavern-style scapece").

Difficulty

TREVISO-STYLE RADICCHIO
RADICCHIO ALLA TREVIGIANA

Preparation time: 15 minutes + 10 minutes cooking time

Ingredients for 4 servings

radicchio trevigiano (Treviso radicchio)
  1 1/3 lbs (600 g)
extra-virgin olive oil   2 tbsp (30 ml)
sage and rosemary   to taste or about
  1 tsp (0.7 g) of each, chopped
salt and pepper   to taste

Method

Wash and prepare the radicchio, remove the outer leaves, and cut it into four sections. Season with salt and pepper, and sprinkle with the sage and rosemary.

Heat the oil in a skillet and add the radicchio. Sauté it on all sides and finish cooking with the lid on until tender, about 10 minutes. Alternatively, you can bake it in the oven at 350° F (180° C) about 10 minutes.

THE TWO TYPES OF RADICCHIO FROM TREVISO

In the province of Treviso in Veneto, there are two types of red radicchio, both of excellent quality, extremely versatile in cooking and used in many dishes from appetizers to desserts.
The so called "early" radicchio has a large elongated head with tight leaves and a small root stub. The leaves are crisp, slightly bitter and suitable for many uses, both raw and cooked. Once the scorching heat of the summer is over, the green leaves of the radicchio are carefully tied together out in the fields so that the heart of the plant is left "in the dark" to develop new bright red leaves that will come through from September onward.
The so-called "late" radicchio, which is the undisputed champion of all the Veneto radicchio, has a tightly bound head of compact regular leaves, which tend to close at the top, and a longish root stub. The leaves are a deep red wine color with slightly pronounced secondary veining, while the white dorsal rib has a pleasantly bitter taste and is very crunchy. This prized radicchio is harvested in November, by which time the fields will have frosted over at least twice. At this point, spring water and the skill of the producers make it flourish to acquire its beautiful appearance, crunchy consistency and special flavor within a few weeks ... to the delight of refined gourmets.

Difficulty

PARMA-STYLE ASPARAGUS

ASPARAGI ALLA PARMIGIANA

Preparation time: 15 minutes + 10 minutes cooking time

Ingredients for 4 servings

asparagus 1 3/4 lbs (800 g)
butter 4 tbsp (60 g)
Parmigiano-Reggiano cheese, grated
  1 3/4 oz (50 g)
salt to taste

Method

Wash the asparagus. Remove the hard ends and cut all the stalks to the same length. Tie them into small bundles and stand them upright in a saucepan of salted water. Boil them, tips upward, about 10 minutes. Cook them to the point that they are still firm (about 10 minutes). Drain and arrange on a serving dish.

Sprinkle the asparagus tips with the grated Parmigiano-Reggiano cheese. Meanwhile, melt the butter in a saucepan. When it is frothy, pour it over the asparagus.

ASPARAGUS RECIPES

Asparagus is a spring vegetable, a flowering perennial plant species which possibly originated in Mesopotamia (the name derives from the Persian sperega, *meaning "shoot"). It was cultivated and used by the Egyptians and by the population of Asia Minor more than 2,000 years ago. Asparagus was indeed very popular with the Ancient Romans, both because of the culinary qualities that make it a true delicacy, and for its medicinal properties: it has a purifying effect on the kidneys and analgesic properties for toothache.*
Today, various types of asparagus are cultivated for culinary purposes. They differ in appearance, flavor and cultivation methods. For example, the white asparagus of Bassano del Grappa which owes its color to the fact that it is cultivated in the absence of light to block natural photosynthesis. The age-old purple asparagus of Albenga is bright purple and relatively large in size. The pink asparagus of Mezzago, the color of whose tips is due to very few hours of exposure to sunlight before picking, or the prized green asparagus of Altedo, which is cultivated in the provinces of Bologna and Ferrara.

Difficulty

SAUTÉED BROCCOLI RABE
CIME DI RAPA SALTATE

Preparation time: 15 minutes + 10 minutes cooking time

Ingredients for 4 servings

broccoli rabe   3 1/3 lbs (1.5 kg),
  cleaned, roughly chopped
extra-virgin olive oil   3 tbsp + 1 tsp
  (50 ml)
garlic   2 cloves, thinly sliced
fresh chili peppers sliced   to taste
salt   to taste

Method

Heat the extra-virgin olive oil in a skillet with the finely sliced garlic and the chili pepper. Cook until the oil is fragrant and the garlic is golden brown. Do not let the garlic brown too much.

Add the chopped broccoli rabe and a pinch of salt and cook for 10 minutes over moderate heat, stirring frequently.

100 PERCENT ITALIAN

Broccoli rabe derives from turnip but is a vegetable in its own right due to its form and color. It is a typically Italian vegetable that was made known all over the world by Italian emigrants at the beginning of the 20th century and is now cultivated and eaten in the United States, Canada and Australia.

In southern Italian cuisine, broccoli rabe is eaten cooked; usually it is simply boiled and dressed with extra-virgin olive oil and lemon juice or with a classic vinaigrette sauce. Alternatively, it can be stewed with chili pepper or combined with broad beans to enhance these legumes with their particular intense flavor and hint of spiciness. Broccoli rabe is also the main ingredient in traditional first courses, including the famous orecchiette pugliesi (typical Apulian pasta shaped like little ears) or the strascinati lucani (typical durum wheat flour pasta shape) with broccoli rabe.

This vegetable is suitable for consumption in fall and winter and is a good source of protein (2.9 oz per 100 oz of edible product); mineral salts such as iron, calcium and phosphorous; vitamins A, B2 and C; and antioxidants. Furthermore, due to its high levels of folate (folic acid), it is recommended for pregnant women.

Difficulty

PICKLED VEGETABLES

GIARDINIERA

Preparation time: 30 minutes + 15 minutes cooking time

Ingredients for 4 servings

cauliflower   1 lb (500 g) about 1 small
   head
carrots   10 1/2 oz (300 g) about
   4 medium
peppers   5 1/3 oz (150 g) about
   1 medium
spring onions   7 oz (200 g)
cucumbers   7 oz (200 g) about
   1 medium
white wine vinegar   2 cups (500 ml)
wild fennel seeds (optional)   to taste
sugar   2 tbsp + 2 tsp (30 g)
peppercorns   to taste
salt   to taste

Method

Prepare and wash all the vegetables. Leave the spring onions whole. Cut the cauliflower into florets, slice the cucumber, cut the peppers into diamond shapes (you can even use a pasta cutter to make special shapes) and cut the carrots into sticks or any other shapes of your choice.

Boil the vinegar with the sugar in a saucepan, add a generous pinch of salt, a couple of peppercorns and some wild fennel seeds to taste.

Boil the different types of vegetables separately in the vinegar, leaving them crunchy.

Put the different vegetables in glass jars, alternating them, and then bring the liquid to the boil again and pour it on the vegetables when it is boiling hot. Close the glass jars and keep them in the refrigerator. Use the giardiniera within a week after you prepare it.

Difficulty

SAUTÉED PEPPERS

PEPERONATA

Preparation time: 15 minutes + 30 minutes cooking time

Ingredients for 4 servings

Bell peppers (preferably a mixture of yellow, red and green) 1 lb (500 g) sliced

yellow onion 3 1/2 oz (100 g) about 1 small, sliced

capers 1 tbsp + 1 tsp (10 g), rinsed and drained

salt-packed anchovies 2, rinsed, drained, and deboned

garlic 1 clove

extra-virgin olive oil 3 tbsp + 2 tsp (50 ml)

salt and pepper to taste

Method

Slice the sliced onion, sauté in a saucepan with the oil together with the whole peeled clove of garlic, the capers and the rinsed and deboned anchovy filets. Wash the peppers, trim, remove the seeds, slice into large pieces and add to the onion and the other ingredients in the saucepan.

Season the mixture with salt and pepper and cook util the peppers have softened and the flavors have melded together, about 20 minutes.

SICILIAN PEPERONATA

Peperonata is a brightly colored dish that is full of flavor and can be served both hot and cold. It is perfect as a side dish but also as an appetizer. It is also a delicious sauce for pasta. It is simple to prepare and its success at the table is guaranteed.
Sicily is the region that boasts the highest number of Peperonata recipes. In Sicily, Peperonata is called "caponata di verdure." The name "caponata" seems to derive from "capone," a Sicilian dialect term for the common dolphin fish or dorado, a fish with particularly prized flesh that, in the past, was served at the tables of the nobility, with a sauce similar to peperonata. Common folk, who could not afford such an expensive fish, replaced it with vegetables.

Difficulty

VEGETABLE CAPONATA
CAPONATA DI VERDURE

Preparation time: 30 minutes + 15 minutes cooking time

Ingredients for 4 servings

extra-virgin olive oil 7 tbsp (100 ml)
eggplant, diced 1/2 lb (250 g) about 1
  small
zucchini, diced 3 1/2 oz (100 g) about 1
  small
celery, chopped 1 3/4 oz (50 g) about
  2 stalks
onion, diced 1 3/4 oz (50 g) about 1/3
  cup
black olives 1 oz (25 g) about 5 olives
salt-packed capers 3/4 oz (20 g),
  rinsed
pine nuts 2 tbsp (15 g)
pistachio nuts 2 tbsp (15 g)
raisins 3 tbsp (15 g)
crushed tomato 3 1/2 oz (100 g)
basil 1 bunch, washed, dried, torn into
  pieces
vinegar 1 tsp (5 ml)
sugar 1 tbsp (10 g)
salt and pepper to taste

Difficulty

Method

Put the diced eggplant in a colander, salt lightly and let it stand until it releases all the bitter juices. Heat 5 tablespoon oil in a skillet over medium-high heat and sauté the eggplant and celery until browned, about 15 minutes.

Heat the remaining oil in a skillet, add the diced onion and sauté until they start to turn brown. Add diced zucchini and sauté lightly.

Add the raisins, rinsed capers, pine nuts and black olives.

Add the crushed tomato and the fried diced eggplant. Season the mixture with salt and pepper and cook for a few minutes. Add the vinegar and sugar and lastly, add a few pistachios and the basil.

THE FAMOUS BRONTE PISTACHIOS

It seems that the pistachio plant, whose gastronomic and therapeutic qualities are mentioned in the Old Testament, originated in the Syrian city of Psitacco. A further confirmation that it was the Arabs who brought and spread pistachios in Sicily is the fact that the Sicilian dialect term given to this oily seed with so many important nutrients is frastuca, which derives from the Arabic frastuch, which in turn derives from the Persian fistich.
Pistachio cultivation reached its height on the island during the second half of the 19th century, at the foot of Mount Etna in the Bronte area. Today this prized Mediterranean specialty is known all over Italy and indeed all over the world: Bronte pistachios are sought after for their aroma in confectionery and ice cream but also for adding flavor to savory dishes such as the quintessentially Sicilian vegetable caponata.

RATATOUILLE
RATATUIA

Preparation time: 10 minutes + 20 minutes cooking time

Ingredients for 4 servings

eggplant   7 oz (200 g) about
    1/3 medium

zucchini   10 1/2 oz (300 g) about 1 1/2
    medium

tomatoes   7 oz (200 g) about 1 1/2
    medium

onions   6 1/3 oz (180 g) about 2 1/2
    small

red bell peppers   3 1/2 oz (100 g)
    about 2 1/2 small

yellow bell peppers   3 1/2 oz (100 g)
    about 1 1/2 small

garlic clove   1

basil leaves, torn into pieces   4

extra-virgin olive oil   1/3 cup + 2 tbsp
    (100 ml)

salt and pepper   to taste

Method

Wash the eggplant, zucchini, tomatoes and peppers and cut them into 3/4 inch (2 cm) cubes. Peel and slice the onions.

Put a pan over medium heat and add the oil, whole garlic clove and onions. Let them soften, then add the peppers. After a few minutes add the eggplant, and finally add the zucchini. Let the vegetables cook for a few minutes, then add the tomatoes and season with salt and pepper. Let everything finish cooking on low heat, until the tomatoes have broken down and the flavors have melded together. Top with basil and serve.

VEGETABLES IN MEDITERRANEAN CULTURE

The ubiquity of vegetables is undoubtedly the element that most inspired Doctor Ancel Keys and his colleagues to outline the nutritional and dietary model known as the "Mediterranean diet." The use of herbs and vegetables of every kind has always been a well-known trait of Italian cooking. One need only consider that Liber de coquina, *which dates to the 13th or perhaps even the 12th century, begins with a series of recipes for vegetables. And after all, cabbage, spinach, fennel and herbs have always been featured players in Italian culinary history.*

Difficulty

BROAD BEANS WITH ANCHOVIES

FAVE ALLE ACCIUGHE

Preparation time: 10 minutes + 30 minutes cooking time

Ingredients for 4 servings

broad beans, fresh (fava beans) 2 1/4 lb
  (1 kg)
garlic 2 cloves chopped
fresh marjoram 1 pinch
anchovies, chopped 4
extra-virgin olive oil 3 tbsp + 2 tsp
  (50 ml)
3 tbsp (40 ml)
vinegar to taste
salt and pepper to taste

Method

Boil the broad beans in a small quantity of salted water until they are cooked al dente. Meanwhile, prepare a sauce by mixing together the chopped anchovies, garlic, marjoram, vinegar, oil, salt and pepper. Drain the beans and toss immediately with the sauce. Serve immediately.

There is a variant: Fresh broad beans blanched in boiling salted water and then seasoned with chopped garlic, oil, marjoram, salt and pepper.

Another sauce can be made using fresh chopped chives, olive oil, salt and pepper.

Difficulty

STIR-FRIED ROMAN CHICORY WITH ANCHOVY SAUCE
PUNTARELLE SALTATE CON SALSA DI ALICI

Preparation time: 15 minutes + 10 minutes cooking time

Ingredients for 4 servings

puntarelle (chicory shoots) 3 1/3 lbs (1.5 kg), roughly chopped
extra-virgin olive oil 3 tbsp + 2 tsp (50 ml)
salt-packed anchovies 2, rinsed, drained, and deboned
garlic 2 cloves, thinly sliced
sliced hot chili pepper to taste
salt to taste

Method

Rinse and debone the anchovies.

Heat the extra-virgin olive oil in a skillet with the finely sliced garlic, anchovies and chili pepper. Do not let the garlic brown too much but cook the mixture until the anchovy has broken into pieces. Add the chopped puntarelle and a pinch of salt.

Cook over moderate heat, stirring frequetly, until the chicory is wilted, about 10 minutes.

A TYPICAL ROMAN SIDE DISH

Puntarelle flavored with anchovies is a simple and tasty side dish that is typical of Roman cuisine. According to tradition this dish is prepared with catalogna frastagliata, chicory shoots from Gaeta (known as "puntarelle"), so this recipe is especially common in Latium and Campania where this plant can easily be found.
It would appear that a fresh salad of puntarelle with an oil, vinegar and anchovy dressing was served as far back as the times of the ancient Romans. Records of that period report that people were very partial to the inner leaves of catalogna frastagliata chicory. It is crunchy and has a pleasant, slightly bitter taste. The best way to serve it raw is to separate it into thin strips and soak them in ice cold water to make them curl up and to partially alleviate the slightly bitter taste.

Difficulty

RADICCHIO WITH SPECK
INSALATA CON SPECK

Preparation time: 10 minutes + 5 minutes cooking time

Ingredients for 4 servings

heads red radicchio   2
speck (or smoked bacon)   7 oz (200 g)
balsamic vinegar   2 tbsp (30 ml)
olive oil   2 tbsp (30 ml)
salt   to taste

Method

Wash and dry the radicchio. Dice the speck and sauté it in the oil in a pan. When the speck is golden brown, add the balsamic vinegar and let it evaporate. Use this sauce to dress the radicchio, seasoning with salt and pepper. Serve immediately.

Difficulty

DID YOU KNOW THAT...

Speck is a type of uncooked seasoned ham that has been aged and lightly smoked. It is typical of the region of Alto Adige, and more specifically of the province of Bolzano. The meat has a characteristically bright pink color, with occasional veins of white fat. It is flat in shape and tastes of a harmonious mixture of salt, spices and smoke.

BAKED STUFFED VEGETABLES
VERDURE RIPIENE AL FORNO

Preparation time: 30 minutes + 30 minutes cooking time

Ingredients for 4 servings

ground beef   1/4 lb (100 g)
Parmigiano-Reggiano cheese, grated
   1 3/4 oz (50 g) about 1/4 cup
eggs   2
bread crumbs   1 3/4 oz (50 g) about
   generous 1/3 cup
zucchini   14 oz (400 g) about 2
yellow peppers   5 1/3 oz (150 g) about
   2 small
tomatoes   1 lb (500 g) about 4 small
extra-virgin olive oil   3 1/2 tbsp (50 ml)
salt, pepper and nutmeg   to taste

Method

Wash the zucchini and trim off ends, then steam until just tender, about 8 minutes. Cut the zucchini lengthwise and scrape out the flesh including the seeds with a teaspoon or a melon baller. Chop the zucchini pulp and set aside.

Wash and dry the tomatoes, then cut the tops off and scoop out the pulp. Chop the tomato pulp and set aside. Prepare the peppers, wash and dry them and then cut them in half and remove seeds.

Heat three-quarters of the oil in a skillet, add the ground beef and sauté until browned. Add the chopped zucchini and tomato pulp and cook for a few minutes to evaporate the excess liquid. Season with salt and pepper.

Transfer the mixture to a bowl and set aside to cool. Add the eggs, half of the grated Parmigiano cheese and the bread crumbs. Adjust the salt and pepper to taste and add a pinch of nutmeg.

Fill the vegetables with the mixture using a spoon or a pastry bag, then place them on a greased baking tray and sprinkle with the remaining Parmigiano cheese and a drop of extra-virgin olive oil.

Bake in the oven at 350° F (180° C) for about 30 minutes. Serve the baked stuffed vegetables hot or cold, as you prefer

Difficulty

VEGETABLES AU GRATIN
VERDURE GRATINATE

Preparation time: 30 minutes + 20 minutes cooking time

Ingredients for 4 servings

FOR THE VEGETABLES:
cauliflower   5 1/3 oz (150 g)
leeks   5 1/3 oz (150 g)
Brussels sprouts   5 1/3 oz (150 g)

FOR THE BÉCHAMEL:
butter   1/2 stick (60 g)
flour   1/3 cup (40 g)
milk   2 cups (1/2 l)
Parmigiano-Reggiano cheese, grated
  1 3/4 oz (50 g)
salt and nutmeg   to taste

Method

Wash the cauliflower, leeks and Brussels sprouts. Cut the cauliflower into florets and remove the roots and green parts of the leeks as well as any damaged outer leaves of the sprouts.

Boil the vegetables separately in salted water until they can be easily pierced with a knife. Drain them and let them cool.

In the meantime prepare the béchamel by melting 3 tablespoons of the butter in a small saucepan, whisking in the flour. Cook for 1-2 minutes over a low flame until the mixture turns yellow. In a small saucepan, boil the milk, whisk it into the butter and flour, bring to boil again and let it boil for one minute. Add salt and flavor with a tiny pinch of nutmeg.

Grease a few individual oven dishes (or a single oven dish) with the remaining butter, place the vegetables in them and pour béchamel over them. Cover them with grated Parmigiano cheese and a little melted butter.

Cook the vegetables in the oven at 350° F (180° C) for 20 minutes or until a golden crust forms on top.

Difficulty

BROAD BEAN FRITTERS

PANELLE DI FAVE

Preparation time: 12 hours soaking time + 3 hours and 30 minutes cooking time

Ingredients for 4 servings

broad beans   2 1/4 lbs (1 kg)
water
salt   to taste
onion, cut into thick slices   1
wild fennel   to taste
extra-virgin olive oil   to taste
frying oil   as needed
chili peppers   to taste

Method

Soak the dried broad beans overnight. The morning after, boil the beans, onion (cut into thick slices) and a few wild fennel tops in enough salted water to cover by 1 inch. Cook for at least 2-3 hours, so that the broad beans become a purée.

Pass the mixture through a sieve and place the thick mixture on a marble board or a flat, well-greased cooking surface. Roll the mixture out into an even sheet about 0.8 inch (2 cm) thick using a rolling pin. Allow to cool and cut into strips, then fry them in hot oil.

Serve hot. If desired sprinkle with crushed chili to taste.

Difficulty

JEWISH-STYLE ARTICHOKES

CARCIOFI ALLA GIUDEA

Preparation time: 20 minutes + 25 minutes cooking time

Ingredients for 4 servings

globe artichokes about 20 4/5 oz
  (600 g) 4 medium
lemon 1
extra-virgin olive oil 1/3 cup (80 ml)
salt and pepper to taste

Method

Remove the hard outer leaves of the artichokes, and cut the stem, leaving about 1 inch (3 cm).

With a very sharp knife, trim all around the head of each artichoke in such a way as to remove just the hard part of the leaves. Soak them in water with lemon juice so they do not turn black.

In a large skillet, heat olive oil to about 270° F (130° C). There should be enough oil to cover the artichokes.

Drain the artichokes of excess water, dry them and then flatten them slightly on a chopping board by pressing on the base so the leaves spread out. Sprinkle a pinch of salt and pepper inside the leaves that are no longer tightly closed.

Slip the artichokes into the skillet and fry them for about 20 minutes or until you can easily insert a knife in the flesh. Drain the artichokes on paper towels.

Just before serving, raise the temperature of the oil to about 350° F (180° C) and return the artichokes to the skillet for 3-5 minutes to make them crunchy.

Drain on paper towels and serve hot.

Difficulty

FRIED VEGETABLES
FRITTO DI VERDURE

Preparation time: 30 minutes + 5 minutes cooking time

Ingredients for 4 servings

zucchini   5 1/3 oz (150 g) about
  1 medium
bell peppers   5 1/3 oz (150 g) about
  2 small
eggplant   5 1/3 oz (150 g) about
  1 small
red onions, preferably Tropea   5 1/3 oz
  (150 g) about 2 small
squash blossoms   1 3/4 oz (50 g)
milk   3/4 cup + 2 tbsp (200 ml)
flour   1 2/3 cups (200 g)
extra-virgin olive oil   to taste
salt   to taste

Method

Clean and peel the vegetables and cut all except the squash blossoms into thin strips. Heat an inch of oil, or a little more, in a large pot over medium heat until shimmering.

Dip all the vegetables and the whole squash blossoms in the milk. Dredge them in the flour, shake off the excess and fry them in the oil.

When they've turned golden brown, remove them with a perforated spoon and place them on paper towels to dry.

Sprinkle them with salt and serve very hot.

VEGETABLE GARDENS

Perhaps the most prominent feature of Mediterranean cuisine, particularly Italian cuisine, is the omnipresence of vegetables. Whether they're wild herbs, roots or garden vegetables, the importance of this component is irrefutable. This characteristic was noted by Giacomo Castelvetro, an intellectual and a man of letters who fled to England after being accused of heresy during the Counter-Reformation. Far from his homeland, he missed the use of vegetables and salads in everyday cooking and pondered the reasons why Italians used those items so much. According to Castelvetro, the first reason has to do with the economic nature and production of Italian terrain, which wasn't made for large-scale breeding. The second reason has to do with climate – the heat and sun of the Italian peninsula aren't conducive to consuming large quantities of meat. These objective geomorphological, economic and structural factors influenced individual and collective tastes, which became subjective, symbolic and cultural over time.

Difficulty

DESSERTS

CHAPTER FIVE

MOSCATO JELLY WITH MIXED BERRIES

GELATINA AL MOSCATO CON FRUTTI DI BOSCO

Preparation time: 10 minutes + 2 hours to set

Ingredients for 4 servings

Moscato wine 1 1/2 cups + 1 tbsp (375 ml)
gelatin sheets 4
alternatively 1 envelope granulated gelatin (0,25 oz)
mixed berries 1 cup (125 g)
mint leaves 4

Method

Soak the gelatin in cold water. When it's softened, remove from the water and squeeze out any excess liquid, if you have used the gelatin sheets. Transfer it to a small pot and let it dissolve in a few tablespoons of warmed Moscato, then stir in the remaining wine. Place a portion of mixed berries and fresh mint leaves in individual serving bowls or glasses and pour the liquid over them.

Refrigerate for at least 2 hours then serve.

Difficulty

GELATIN

The ancient Egyptians likely produced a precursor to gelatin, but it was in the 17th century that the process for making foods – sweet or savory – with that peculiar gelatinous consistency was officially defined. In the pre-modern era, the substances used to obtain similar results were mostly of animal origin: pork rinds, bovine skins, and bones from various animals. Some cookbooks even mention "grated deer antlers." In any case, the recipe for gelatin was born in the realm of the apothecary, halfway between gastronomy, pharmacology, and alimentary alchemy.

COLD ZABAGLIONE WITH MOSCATO
ZABAIONE FREDDO AL MOSCATO

Preparation time: 15 minutes + 10 minutes cooking time + 2 hours resting time

Ingredients for 4 servings

egg yolks   4
sugar   2 tbsp (25 g)
Moscato d'Asti or other Moscato wine
   generous 3/4 cup (200 ml)
cream   7/8 cup (220 ml)
one envelope gelatin dissolved in 1 cup
   warm water

Method

In a pan, preferably copper, beat the egg yolks lightly with the sugar and wine. Place the pan over low heat (or in a bain-marie) and continue cooking until the mixture becomes frothy and has thickened. Meanwhile, prepare the gelatin according to package instructions and add to the pan.

Remove from the heat and leave to cool. When the mixture is cool, whip the cream and carefully fold it into the cooled zabaglione. Pour into individual bowls and chill in the refrigerator for at least 2 hours.

Garnish to taste.

Difficulty

STUFFED PEACHES
PESCHE RIPIENE

Preparation time: 20 minutes + 30 minutes cooking time

Ingredients for 4 servings

peaches   2.2 lbs (1 kg) about 8 medium
skinless almonds   4 1/5 oz (120 g)
bread roll, soaked in milk   1
eggs, separated   3
sugar   5 1/3 oz (150 g)
confectioner's sugar for serving   1 3/4 oz
   (50 g)

Method

Choose peaches that are not too ripe. Cut in half, and using a pointed knife, remove the pit and a bit of the flesh, in order to create a space for the filling. Put the peaches in a greased oven dish. Prepare the filling. Wring out the milk-soaked bread. Whisk the egg yolks with the sugar. Crush the almonds in a mortar and mix them with the bread, the peach flesh and the egg/sugar mixture.

Beat the egg whites until they form stiff peaks, then fold them into the filling mixture. Fill the peaches with the mixture and bake for about 30 minutes at 300° F (150° C). Dust with confectioner's sugar and serve lukewarm.

The almonds can be replaced with chopped macaroons as a variation.

Difficulty

DID YOU KNOW THAT...

Originating in China, where they are a symbol of immortality, peaches were brought to the Western world by Alexander the Great.

VANILLA SEMIFREDDO

SEMIFREDDO ALLA VANIGLIA

Preparation time: 1 hour + 3 hours freezing time

Ingredients for 4 servings

egg semifreddo base (see below)
  8 1/2 oz (250 g)
cream, partially whipped 2 generous
  cups (500 ml)
Italian-style meringue (see below)
  5 oz (140 g)

FOR THE EGG SEMIFREDDO BASE:
egg yolks 7 tbsp (100 g)
sugar 2/3 cup (130 g)
water 2 1/2 tbsp (35 ml)
gelatin 1 1/2 packets
split vanilla bean 1

FOR THE ITALIAN-STYLE MERINGUE:
egg whites about 4 tbsp (50 g)
sugar 1/2 cup (100 g)
water 4 tsp (20 ml)

Method

To prepare the Italian-style meringue, put 5 tablespoon sugar and the water in a pan and place over medium heat. Meanwhile, beat the whites with the rest of the sugar until they form stiff peaks.

When the sugar mixture has reached 250° F (120° C), gradually beat into the stiffly beaten egg-whites and continue beating until the mixture is well combined. Put aside.

Prepare the gelatin according to package instructions.

For the semifreddo base, cook the sugar with the water, as for the meringue, then quickly beat in the egg yolks. Add the prepared gelatin, scrape the vanilla bean into it and continue beating until the mixture has cooled completely. Fold together the meringue and semifreddo base, incorporate the partially whipped unsweetened cream. Pour into molds and place in the freezer for 3 hours.

Remove from the molds and serve.

Difficulty

CITRUS FRUIT SOUP WITH PISTACHIOS

ZUPPETTA DI AGRUMI AI PISTACCHI

Preparation time: 30 minutes

Ingredients for 4 servings

oranges 10 1/2 oz (300 g) about 2 medium

yellow grapefruit 5 1/3 oz (150 g) about 1 medium

pink grapefruit 5 1/3 oz (150 g) about 1 medium

mandarin oranges 7 oz (200 g) about 2 medium

shelled, peeled, and chopped unsalted pistachios 1/4 cup (30 g)

sugar 2 tbsp (25 g)

Method

Use a potato peeler to zest 1 orange, half a yellow grapefruit and half a pink grapefruit. Be careful not to get any of the bitter white pith. Slice the peels into thin strips.

Fill a small pot with water and bring to a boil. Add the peels and, as soon as the water returns to a boil, turn off the heat. Remove the boiled peels with a slotted spoon, and add the sugar and a few tablespoons of citrus fruit juice to the water. Bring it to a boil, then turn off the heat and let it cool. Set aside.

Using a small, very sharp knife separate the fruit segments from the membrane, except for the mandarin oranges (these you can simply peel and separate the segments.) Reserve any juice from this process. In a bowl, toss together the fruit syrup, fruit segments, and any fruit juice. Chill. When thoroughly chilled, and divide among individual bowls or cups. Garnish with reserved fruit peel and top with pistachios.

Difficulty

LEMON MOUSSE WITH EXTRA-VIRGIN OLIVE OIL
MOUSSE DI LIMONI CON OLIO EXTRA-VERGINE DI OLIVA

Preparation time: 30 minutes + 2 hours to set

Ingredients for 4 servings

MERINGUE:

sugar   1/3 cup + 2 tsp (80 g)
egg whites   2 tbsp + 2 tsp (40 g)
water   1 tbsp + 1 tsp (20 ml)

MOUSSE:

heavy cream   2/3 cup + 1 tbsp (170 ml)
lemon juice   1/4 cup + 2 tsp (70 ml)
gelatin sheets   2
extra-virgin olive oil   1 tbsp + 1 tsp
  (20 ml)

Method

Start by making the meringue. Heat the water in a small pot with 1/3 cup of sugar. Beat the egg whites with the remaining sugar in a bowl. You can use a whisk, but a beater or a stand mixer would be better. When the mix sugar and water reaches 250° F (120° C), slowly add it to the egg whites and keep beating until it cools.

Soak the gelatin in cold water for 5 minutes, then slowly dissolve it over low heat or in the microwave.

Whip the heavy cream and fold it into the meringue along with the gelatin and lemon juice.

Pour the mixture into molds and freeze them for a couple of hours, or until they set. Transfer the mousse from the molds to serving plates and drizzle it with extra-virgin olive oil.

Difficulty

STRAWBERRY SORBET
SORBETTO DI FRAGOLA

Preparation time: 20 minutes + 3 hours to freeze

Ingredients for 4 servings

strawberries 8 oz (250 g)
water 1 cup (250 ml)
sugar 3/4 cup + 3 tbsp (185 g)
lemon 1/4

Method

Rinse the strawberries. Wash the lemon; cut it into quarters and squeeze the juice from 1 quarter.

Blend the strawberries with the water and sugar. Add the lemon juice.

Refrigerate the mixture until completely chilled at least 3 hours. Transfer it to an ice cream maker and let it run until the sorbet reaches a uniform consistency.

THE ANCIENT TASTE FOR SORBET

The custom of eating snow flavored with fruit is very ancient. Athenaeus of Naucratus, a writer from the 2nd-3rd century AD, described a cold drink flavored with pomegranate in the Deipnosofistae, and Pliny the Younger mentions a frozen cream made with eggs, milk, and honey. These ancient texts tell us that the taste for cold treats dates very far back in time. But it was in the 16th century – helped by the diffusion of sugarcane through the Arabs – that sorbets reached their peak on the tables of the powerful. At the time, every castle and palace had an icehouse (an underground depository or small artificial hill where snow from the nearest mountains, gathered in winter, was stored and preserved). Bartolomeo Scappi provided the first recipe for Italian sorbet in his Opera (1570). In the 17th century, actual sorbet shops were opened (mostly in Venice and Naples) and it started to reach a larger percentage of the population. Contemporary technology did not spark a new desire for sweet, cold delicacies, but simply made it possible for everyone to have some.

Difficulty

COFFEE GRANITA
GRANITA AL CAFFÈ

Preparation time: 20 minutes + 2 hours to freeze

Ingredients for 4 servings

espresso   2/3 cup (150 ml)
water   1 cup (255 ml)
sugar   2/3 cup (100 g)

Method

Dissolve the sugar in the hot coffee, then add the water and let the liquid cool. Pour it into a bowl and put it in the freezer.

From time to time, mix the granita with a whisk, breaking up any parts that may have started to freeze. Continue doing this until you are left with a homogeneous granita.

Remove from the freezer and serve in four individual bowls.

THE ENERGY OF THE SUFIS

Coffee was imported to Europe from South America by the conquistadors. It is the drink obtained by grinding the seeds of some species of small tropical bushes of the Coffea genus, members of the Rubiaceae family. The types of coffee that are most common today, differing in taste and caffeine content, are Arabica (Coffea arabica), native to Ethiopia, southeastern Sudan, northern Kenya and Yemen (where the first historical records exist of the consumption of this drink by followers of Sufism in 1450); Robusta (Coffea canephora) from tropical Africa; and to a lesser extent Liberica (Coffea liberica), native of Liberia.

Difficulty

ORANGE GRANITA
GRANITA ALL'ARANCIA

Preparation time: 20 minutes + 4 hours to freeze

Ingredients for 4 servings

water   1 cup (250 ml)
sugar   1/4 cup + 2 tbsp (75 g)
lemon juice   3 tbsp + 2 tsp (50 ml)
orange juice   2/3 cup (150 ml)
grated zest of oranges   2

Method

Carefully wash the oranges and grate the zest of both, being careful not to get any of the bitter white part. Then juice them, filtering the juice with a fine mesh strainer.

Make a syrup by boiling the water and sugar for 4 to 5 minutes. Let it cool and combine it with the citrus juices and orange peel.

Freeze the liquid for about 1 hour, until ice crystals start to form. Whisk it well and put it back in the freezer. Repeat this process at least 4 or 5 times. The granita is ready when the ice reaches a uniform consistency and granularity.

Difficulty

VANILLA, CHOCOLATE AND STRACCIATELLA ICE CREAM
GELATO STRACCIATELLA, CIOCCOLATO E CREMA

Preparation time: 20 minutes + 6 hours freezing time

Ingredients for approximately 2 pints (900 ml) of ice cream

STRACCIATELLA:
milk   2 1/8 cups (500 ml)
sugar   scant 2/3 cup (120 g)
powdered skim milk   2 2/3 tbsp (20 g)
dextrose   1/2 oz (15 g)
stabilizer   1/8 oz (3.5 g)
cream   5 tbsp (75 g)
semi-sweet chocolate   as needed

CHOCOLATE:
milk   2 1/8 cups (500 ml)
sugar   2/3 cup (130 g)
unsweetend cocoa   1 3/4 oz (50 g)
dextrose   1/2 oz (15 g)
stabilizer   1/8 oz (3.5 g)
semi-sweet chocolate   1/3 oz (10 g)

VANILLA:
milk   2 1/8 cups (500 ml)
egg yolks   3
sugar   3/4 cup (150 g)
dextrose   1/2 oz (20 g)
powdered skim milk   2 2/3 tbsp (15 g)
stabilizer   1/8 oz (3.5 g)
cream   5 tbsp (50 g)
vanilla bean   1

Difficulty

Method

Stracciatella

Heat the milk to 115° F (45° C) in a saucepan. Mix the sugar, powdered milk, dextrose and stabilizer and pour the dry mixture in a steady stream into the milk. Heat the milk to 150° F (65° C), add the cream and heat. Cool rapidly to 40° F (4° C) by putting the mixture in a container and immersing it in a bowl of water and ice. Refrigerate for six hours and then freeze in an ice cream machine, stirring until the mixture is no longer frothy but looks dry and not glossy (the time it takes depends on the ice cream machine used). As soon as the ice cream is ready, mix in the chopped semi-sweet chocolate.

Chocolate

Heat the milk to 115° F (45° C) in a saucepan. Mix sugar, unsweetened cocoa, dextrose and stabilizer and pour the dry mixture in a steady stream into the milk. Heat to 150° F (65° C) and add the semi-sweet chocolate. Cool rapidly to 40° F (4° C) by putting the mixture in a container and immersing it in a bowl of water and ice. Refrigerate for six hours and then freeze in an ice cream machine, stirring until the mixture is no longer frothy but looks dry and not glossy (the time it takes depends on the ice-cream machine used).

Vanilla

Heat the milk with the cracked vanilla bean to 115° F (45° C) and then remove the vanilla bean. Mix the sugar, powdered milk, dextrose and stabilizer and pour the dry mixture in a steady stream into the milk. Heat to 150° F (65° C), and add the cream. Cool rapidly by putting the mixture in a container and immersing it in a bowl of water and ice. Refrigerate for six hours and then freeze in an ice cream machine, stirring until the mixture is no longer frothy but looks dry and not glossy (the time it takes depends on the ice-cream machine used).

PEACHES STUFFED WITH AMARETTI COOKIES
PESCHE RIPIENE ALL'AMARETTO

Preparation time: 20 minutes + 30 minutes cooking time

Ingredients for 4 servings

peaches 1 lbs (500 kg) about 4 medium
amaretti cookies, crushed 3 1/2 oz
 (100 g) about 5
unsweetened cocoa 3 tbsp + 2 tsp (20 g)
eggs, separated 2
sugar 1/4 cup + 2 tbsp (70 g)

Method

Wash the peaches and cut them in half. Remove the pits and use a spoon to scoop out a bit more flesh from the middle. Chop the flesh and mix it with the 2 egg yolks, hand-crushed amaretti and cocoa. Beat the egg whites with the sugar until stiff peaks form. Fold them into the other mixture you prepared.

Fill the peach halves, arrange them in a pan lined with parchment paper and bake them at 325° F (160° C) until the peaches are tender, about 30 minutes.

Serve them warm or cold, according to preference.

THE FOOD OF THE GODS

The Aztecs believed that the winged serpent Quetzalcoatl gave man the cacao plant, a divine gift that was central to religious, economic, and ritual life of those lands. Cacao was actually considered a panacea, a cure for illnesses of both the mind and body. The Native American drank beverages made from cacao mixed with other ingredients, which Gerolamo Benzoni called "a drink more suited to pigs than humans." No impression has ever been so wrong. Cacao was first recorded in Europe in 1544, when a delegation of indigenous nobles offered the king of Spain a dark, dense drink called xocoatl. The first shipment of cacao beans arrived at the port of Seville in 1585 and the Europeans began enjoying hot drinks made from cacao aromatized with spices, vanilla, citrus peels, and (this was the definitive step) refined by the addition of sugar. Drinking cups of chocolate became a trend, and there were even chocolate houses that existed specifically for consuming this delicacy. And from there, cacao continued its victory march unhindered.

CHOCOLATE-COVERED ORANGE PEELS
SCORZETTE D'ARANCIA RICOPERTE DI CIOCCOLATO

Preparation time: 30 minutes + 12 hours to dry

Ingredients for 4 servings

FOR THE PEELS:
candied orange peel in quarters   4 1/2 oz (130 g)

FOR THE GLAZE:
dark chocolate   2 1/2 oz (70 g)

Method

Arrange the candied orange peel quarters on a wire rack and leave to dry at room temperature overnight.

The next day, cut the orange peels into strips about 1/4 inch (5-6 mm) wide and temper the dark chocolate: melt the chocolate in a bain-marie or microwave at 110-120° F (45-50° C) (use a cooking thermometer), then pour one-third to one-half onto a marble surface. Let this cool until it reaches 80° F (25° C), then add it on top of the remaining hot chocolate. When the temperature of this new mixture reaches 90° F (30° C), it is ready to be used.

Glaze the candied orange peels in tempered chocolate using a fork.

Drain the excess chocolate and place the frosted sticks on a sheet of parchment paper.

Let the chocolate-covered orange peels crystallize at room temperature.

Difficulty

ALPHABETIC INDEX OF RECIPES

INGREDIENTS INDEX

233

All photographs are by
ACADEMIA BARILLA

ACADEMIA BARILLA

In the heart of Parma, one of the most distinguished capitals of Italian cuisine, is the Barilla Center. Set in the grounds of the former Barilla pasta factory, this modern architectural complex is the home of Academia Barilla. This was founded in 2004 to promote the art of Italian cuisine, protecting the regional gastronomic heritage and safeguarding it from imitations and counterfeits, while encouraging the great traditions of the Italian restaurant industry. Academia Barilla is also a center of great professionalism and talent that is exceptional in the world of cooking. It organizes cooking classes for culinary enthusiasts, it provides services for those involved in the restaurant industry, and it offers products of the highest quality. In 2007, Academia Barilla was awarded the "Premio Impresa-Cultura" for its campaigns promoting the culture and creativity of Italian gastronomy throughout the world. The center was designed to meet the training requirements of the world of food and it is equipped with all the multimedia facilities necessary for organizing major events. The remarkable gastronomic auditorium is surrounded by a restaurant, a laboratory for sensory analysis, and various teaching rooms equipped with the most modern technology. The Gastronomic Library contains over 10,000 books and a remarkable collection of historic menus as well as prints related to culinary subjects. The vast cultural heritage of the library can be consulted on the internet which provides access to hundreds of digitized historic texts. This avant-garde approach and the presence of a team of internationally famous experts enables Academia Barilla to offer a wide range of courses, meeting the needs of both restaurant chefs and amateur food lovers. In addition, Academia Barilla arranges cultural events and activities aiming to develop the art of cooking, supervised by experts, chefs, and food critics, that are open to the public. It also organizes the "Academia Barilla Film Award", for short films devoted to Italy's culinary traditions.

www.academiabarilla.com

METRIC EQUIVALENTS

LIQUID/DRY MEASURES	
U.S.	**METRIC**
¼ teaspoon	1.25 milliliters
½ teaspoon	2.5 milliliters
1 teaspoon	5 milliliters
1 tablespoon (3 teaspoons)	15 milliliters
1 fluid ounce (2 tablespoons)	30 milliliters
¼ cup	60 milliliters
⅓ cup	80 milliliters
½ cup	120 milliliters
1 cup	240 milliliters
1 pint (2 cups)	480 milliliters
1 quart (4 cups; 32 ounces)	960 milliliters
1 gallon (4 quarts)	3.84 liters
1 ounce (by weight)	28 grams
1 pound	454 grams
2.2 pounds	1 kilogram